GUITAR *signature licks*

Robert Johnson™

A STEP-BY-STEP BREAKDOWN OF THE LEGENDARY GUITARIST'S STYLE AND TECHNIQUE

by DAVE RUBIN

Cover Photography ©1989 Delta Haze Corporation
Used by Permission
The Robert Johnson signature is a ® Registered Trademark of
Delta Haze Corporation and Claud Johnson

ISBN 0-7935-8921-5

7777 W. BLUEMOUND RD. P.O. BOX 13819 MILWAUKEE, WI 53213

Copyright © 2000 by HAL LEONARD CORPORATION
International Copyright Secured   All Rights Reserved

For all works contained herein:
Unauthorized copying, arranging, adapting, recording or
public performance is an infringement of copyright.
Infringers are liable under the law.

Visit Hal Leonard Online at
www.halleonard.com

Audio Credits:
Guitar parts on the accompanying CD
recorded by Doug Boduch
at Beat House, Milwaukee, WI

CONTENTS

PAGE	TITLE	CD TRACK
4	Introduction	
5	The Tunings	
5	Robert Johnson's Arrangements	
6	The Fingerstyle Technique of Robert Johnson	
7	The Guitars	
8	Kind Hearted Woman Blues	1-3
12	I Believe I'll Dust My Broom	4
15	Sweet Home Chicago	5-6
18	Ramblin' On My Mind	7-8
21	Come On In My Kitchen	9-12
25	Terraplane Blues	13-15
29	32-20 Blues	16-19
33	Cross Road Blues (Crossroads)	20-23
40	Walkin' Blues	24-26
44	Preachin' Blues (Up Jumped The Devil)	27-28
48	If I Had Possession Over Judgment Day	29-30
52	I'm A Steady Rollin' Man (Steady Rollin' Man)	31-32
55	Hell Hound On My Trail	33-34
58	Stop Breakin' Down Blues	35-36
60	Love In Vain Blues	37
62	Guitar Notation Legend	

INTRODUCTION

Virtually the entire history of Delta blues had been written before Robert Johnson made his landmark recordings in 1936 and 1937. W.C. Handy, the "Father of the Blues," had given credible witness in 1903 by describing a slide guitarist at the Tutwiler, Mississippi train station and Charlie Patton seems to have been one of the first to be recognized for playing the blues around 1907. Recordings by country blues guitarists Papa Charlie Jackson (1924), Freddie Spruell (1926), Blind Lemon Jefferson (1926), Blind Blake (1926), Sylvester Weaver, and Walter Beasley (1927) led to Tommy Johnson (1928) as the beginning of Mississippi Delta blues. Ten years later when Robert Johnson met his tragic and violent end, the Delta blues era was over. Since the advent of the electric guitar in 1936, the movement towards blues *bands* in the early forties and away from solo acoustic country blues artists had begun, never to be reversed.

Fate intervened by way of Johnson's death in two profound ways. Besides depriving the world of a singularly brilliant musician, it possibly changed the course of country blues and urban blues history. The legendary promoter and record producer John Hammond was planning a concert called *From Spirituals to Swing* at Carnegie Hall in New York City for the winter of 1938, and wanted Johnson as the example of Delta blues. When informed of Johnson's demise, he booked Big Bill Broonzy in his place and played "Walkin' Blues" and "Preachin' Blues" on a phonograph from the stage.

Many stories, some perhaps apocryphal, abound about Johnson's guitar prowess. It is mentioned how he could be in a room with the radio on, seemingly oblivious to the music and then reproduce it note for note at a later time. Johnny Shines told how Johnson moved a juke joint audience of men and women to tears with a rendition of "Come On In My Kitchen." Son House spoke in the sixties about how Johnson's playing improved drastically over a short period of time, giving rise to the "selling of one's soul at the cross roads" story decades after his death. The undisputed truth, however, lies in the twenty-nine titles that are Johnson's entire recorded legacy. Arguably representing the end of the Delta blues era and forecasting the start of what would become electric Chicago blues in the hands of Muddy Waters in the late forties, they are monuments of American music.

Fifteen selections that give hard evidence of Johnson's genius are presented in the following pages. Boogie bass patterns, vibrant dominant chords, perfectly crafted fills, and shimmering slide licks exist in compositions held together by his unmatched ability to juggle three independent guitar parts at one time while *singing*. Singing and *swinging* would be even more accurate as his sense of "blues time" is also the standard, particularly for boogie tunes, that all blues afterwards could be measured.

Blues is the deepest form of American music and Robert Johnson may very well be the deepest blues guitarist of all time. Learning his repertoire should prove to be a profound, moving, and challenging experience.

THE TUNINGS

Robert Johnson's vaunted repertoire, as shown in the selections contained herein, can be grouped in terms of the tunings employed as follows:

Standard Tuning (E–A–D–G–B–E)
1. Kind Hearted Woman Blues
2. Sweet Home Chicago
3. 32-20 Blues
4. I'm A Steady Rollin' Man

Open A Tuning (E–A–E–A–C#–E)
1. Come On In My Kitchen
2. Terraplane Blues
3. Cross Road Blues
4. Walkin' Blues
5. If I Had Possession Over Judgment Day
6. Stop Breakin' Down Blues

Open E Tuning (E–B–E–G#–B–E)
1. Ramblin' On My Mind
2. Preachin' Blues

Open Em Tuning (E–B–E–G–B–E)
1. Hell Hound On My Trail

Open G Tuning (D–G–D–G–B–D)
1. Love In Vain Blues

Aadd 9 - "Mystery Tuning" (E–B–E–A–C#–E)
1. I Believe I'll Dust My Broom

ROBERT JOHNSON'S ARRANGEMENTS

The majority of Robert Johnson's material is based on 12-bar blues progressions. However, within various compositions occur verses of more or less than 12 measures. Often this is the result of Johnson playing a pair of 2/4 measures where one 4/4 measure would normally be expected. In addition, he also plays measures of 3/4, 5/4, and 6/4 time that casually coexist alongside measures of 4/4.

Delta and country blues musicians before World War II, especially when performing solo, felt no compunction to adhere to strict 12, 8 or 16-bar blues arrangements. It was only after the war, when combo blues began to replace the itinerant songsters of old, that set progressions became common.

THE FINGERSTYLE TECHNIQUE OF ROBERT JOHNSON

Robert Johnson was a solo acoustic blues artist. Indeed, some (this author included) would say that he was the *ultimate* acoustic blues guitarist. Therefore, as all of his recordings consist of him and his guitar, similar fingerstyle technique can be applied to all the songs in this book.

LEFT HAND

Johnson had especially long fingers. Combined with the short scale (24 and 3/4 inch) Gibson guitars that he favored, he was able to span great distances on the fingerboard. As opposed to many of his contemporaries, however, he tended not to hook his thumb over the edge of the fingerboard to fret the low E or A string except to play D7/F♯. Instead, he barred across the strings as if using a capo. Usually this involved his index finger, but he also barred on the bottom strings with his middle finger, allowing his index finger to fret notes lower than the barre. Virtually without exception, Johnson used his little to play the root note at fret 12 on string 1 for his descending turnaround patterns.

For the slide pieces Johnson placed a bottleneck on his little finger in order to employ his remaining fingers to fret other notes and patterns. Be prepared to use the slide on the top two or three strings only in some songs, leaving the bass strings open or accessible for the first three fingers of the left hand.

RIGHT HAND

Photographic evidence reveals that Johnson used a plastic thumbpick and bare fingers. Common acoustic fingerstyle practice dictates the thumb thumping along on the bass strings (6, 5, and 4) and the index and middle fingers plucking melodies and ornaments on the treble strings. For much of this material that approach will work well. Be aware, though, that it appears from the recordings that he also attacked the treble strings with his thumbpick to get a sharper, cleaner "flatpick" sound on many occasions. Let your ear and logic be your guide and feel free to adapt your own personal fingering choices to reproduce Johnson's music.

ABOUT THE ARRANGEMENTS

In Johnson's day musicians did not fade out their songs in person or on record. In fact, blues artists before the mid-fifties almost always had definite endings for the compositions. This was particularly true for 12-bar blues. In Johnson's case he generally takes the turnaround, plays it almost exactly as he had been doing, but ends with the tonic (I) chord instead of the V.

THE GUITARS

There are three known photos of Robert Johnson. The two that have been made public show him with two different instruments. Careful, critical listening and research have led to the following conclusions regarding the identification of these guitars and their use on the recordings.

Gibson L-1, circa 1929

Featured in the Studio Portrait where Johnson is nattily attired in a pinstriped suit, the L-1 was introduced in 1926 as a budget flat top. It started out like the less expensive L-0 as a very small bodied-guitar with a narrow waist, and measured 13 and 1/2 inches at the widest point on the lower bout. By 1929 it had grown to 14 and 3/4 inches wide (like the L-2) while still retaining the 12-fret neck. In 1932 it was stretched to 14 frets clear of the body and was summarily discontinued in 1937.

L-1s offered quality construction, balanced tone, playability, and affordability to musicians in the Depression-era South. Thin woods, braces, and finishes contributed to the wonderful responsiveness and resonance of these little beauties. The price to be paid for this featherweight construction, however, is that they will have a tendency to self-destruct if strung with heavy (.013–.056) acoustic strings.

Judging from the sound and the lack of a capo at Johnson's last two sessions in Dallas in 1937, it appears that he used the L-1 on the following titles presented here: "I'm A Steady Rollin' Man," "Hell Hound On My Trail," "Stop Breakin' Down Blues," and "Love In Vain Blues."

Gibson L-00, circa 1935-36

The photo booth self-portrait presents a guitar that is problematic in making a positive identification. It would be helpful if the headstock was visible along with more of the body. In lieu of that, however, the visible evidence points to the 1935-36 Gibson L-00 as the most likely candidate.

Introduced around 1930, the L-00 was a 14-fret guitar with the same body dimensions as other L-series guitars, including the L-1. Initially finished entirely in black lacquer, it acquired a small sunburst in 1934 and back binding in 1937. In addition, these latter models all had a position marker at fret 15. The photo booth picture shows a guitar without back binding or a dot marker at fret 15, matching the 1935-36 L-00 exactly. It also matches 14-fret Kalamazoo guitars (made by Gibson) from the era. However, they were not introduced until 1938, the year of Johnson's passing.

It seems that Johnson used the 14-fret L-00 on the remainder of our selections recorded in San Antonio in four sessions in 1936: "Kind Hearted Woman Blues," "I Believe I'll Dust My Broom," "Sweet Home Chicago," "Ramblin' On My Mind," "Come On In My Kitchen," "Terraplane Blues," "32-20 Blues," "Cross Road Blues," "Walkin' Blues," "Preachin' Blues" and "If I Had Possession Over Judgment Day."

Circa 1929, Gibson L-1

Gibson L-00 or Kalamazoo

KIND HEARTED WOMAN BLUES
SA 2580-1
Words and Music by Robert Johnson
(Recorded Monday, November 23, 1936 in San Antonio, Texas)

Fig. 1—Intro and Verses 1 and 2

"Kind Hearted Woman Blues" is justly renown for containing Johnson's only recorded solo. It was likely one of his oldest and best tunes as he chose it for his first side at his first session. A moderate slow blues delivered with understated passion, it was one of the few "hits" released in his lifetime.

This is a 12-bar blues with a 3-measure intro. Notice that the intro has Johnson's patented "double turnaround" where he uses four-note voicings (I7, I°7 and ivm6) in measure 1 to lead to the I chord in measure 2. Note that this measure of 6/4 time is really a truncated version of two measures of 4/4. Measures 2 and 3 contain his classic descending turnaround with the root on the top (string 1) as a pedal tone.

Verse 1 uses similar chord forms (partial I7 and I°7 chords along with open position inversions) and the same turnaround pattern as measures 2 and 3 of the intro. Verse 2 employs, in measures 1-4, the four-note voicing and triads from measure 1 of the intro. Be aware that verse 2 appears to have 11 measures due to measure 7 of 6/4 time, although it should really be two measures of 4/4.

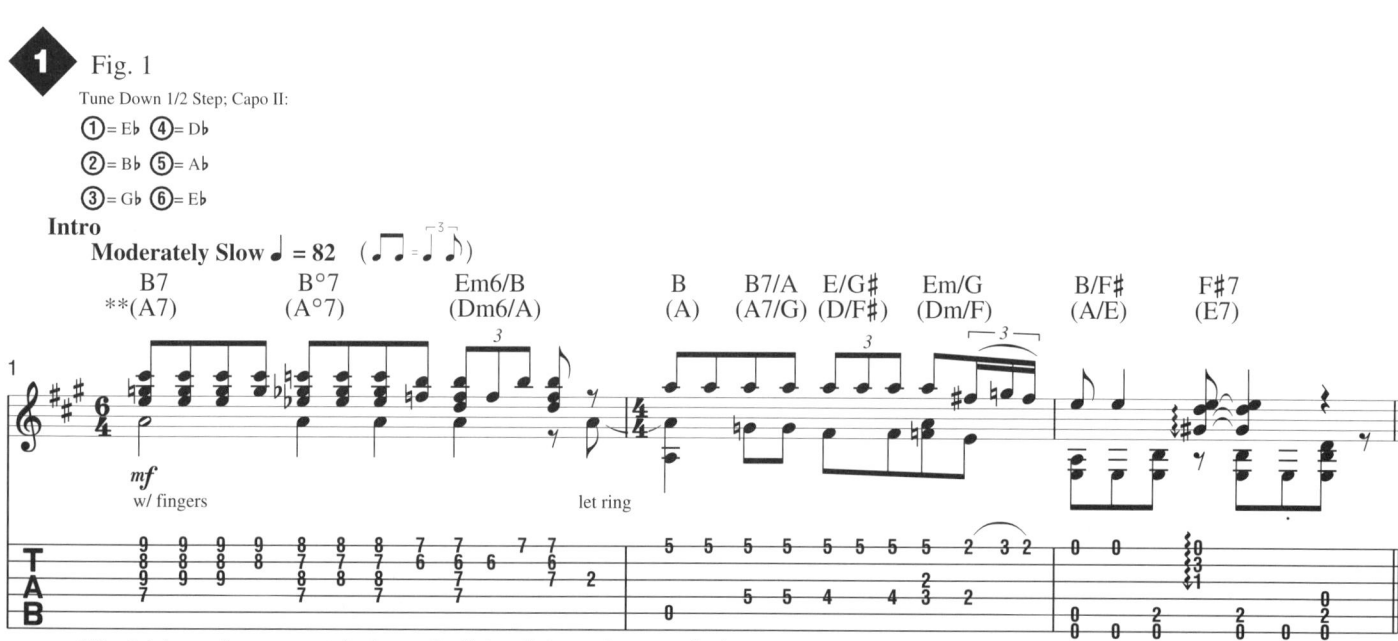

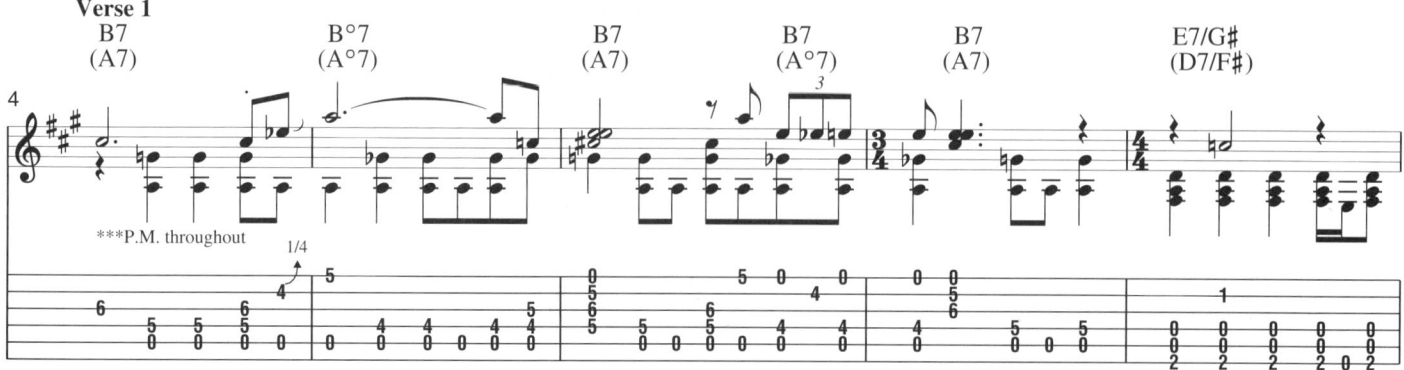

Copyright © (1978), 1990, 1991 King Of Spades Music
All Rights Reserved   Used by Permission

Fig. 2—Bridge

The bridge is also 12 measures long and follows the same arrangement as the verses. Because of the stop-time in measures 1, 2, and 3, however, this section functions as a bridge, beautifully setting up the instrumental break that follows. As in verse 1, Johnson makes the same triple-stop shape on strings 5, 4, and 3 for the implied I7, moving it down one fret to accommodate the I°7. Notice that in the verse he picks the notes from these forms more minimally in a "broken chord" fashion.

Do not miss the exceedingly cool double stops and bends occurring in measures 5 and 6 that imply a 9th chord harmony. Classic blues guitar begins here!

Fig. 3—Solo

Based on the opening 7th chord forms of verse 2, the solo trucks along at a sprightly pace due to the copious triplets on top and the swing eighths on the bottom. Perhaps unconsciously (or due to nerves via his first recording session), Johnson speeds up as "Kind Hearted Woman Blues" progresses. By the time he finishes his solo he has accelerated from a slow blues to a medium shuffle.

Measures 1-4 could be seen as another type of double-turnaround. At any rate, the forward motion engendered by these forms is exhilarating.

I BELIEVE I'LL DUST MY BROOM
SA 2581-1
Words and Music by Robert Johnson
(Recorded Monday, November 23, 1936 in San Antonio, Texas)

Fig. 4—Intro and Verses 1 and 2

"I Believe I'll Dust My Broom" is one of Johnson's greatest songs, an icon of the blues and a landmark Delta blues due to its revolutionary tuning. It is probably the most covered of his compositions, with Elmore James' 1951 epochal electric version topping the list.

Johnson's favorite open tuning was A (low to high: E–A–E–A–C♯–E) and Aadd 9 is only one string different. It is significant, however, as changing string 5 to B (from A in open A tuning) has the effect of placing the root on string 6. This makes the key E instead of A (where the root is on string 5 and the 5th on string 6) and opens up a whole new realm of possibilities. Boogie patterns can be played in open or barre positions while hot licks are simultaneously fingered on the treble strings. This can also be accomplished in open D and E tunings as well, but in Aadd9 harmonies in 3rds, 9ths, and 10ths lay right under the fingers. In addition, the turnarounds are particularly enriched.

The two-measure intro is basically the same turnaround pattern used in measures 11 and 12 of each verse. The verses are similar, although Johnson does throw in subtle variations. This is particularly evident in the I chord "hook" played in measures 1, 2, 3, and 7 of the I chord. Check out the difference in these sections between verses 1 and 2. The addition of the 9th on the top string and hip ♭5th on string 2 to the basic barred double-stop at fret 10 reveals Johnson's ear for telling detail. By the way, in standard or open E tuning, that double stop would require two fingers (ring and index), thereby making the rest of the pattern much more difficult to play, especially at this tempo. Be aware that Johnson alternates the trebly hook with an open, bass string boogie pattern in a dynamic "call-and-response" manner.

The bass string boogie patterns for the IV and V chords are accessed in true Delta blues fashion by moving one's hand position to frets 5 and 7 respectively. Though not indicated on the staff, the best way to play these forms (and a great deal of Robert Johnson's music) is to barre across all six strings. Speaking of barres, note that you must make a partial barre with your middle finger on strings 6 and 5 to play the V9 chord in the intro and all the turnarounds. (Note: "Phonograph Blues" take 2 is based on the same accompaniment as "I Believe I'll Dust My Broom" except that the tempo is considerably faster.)

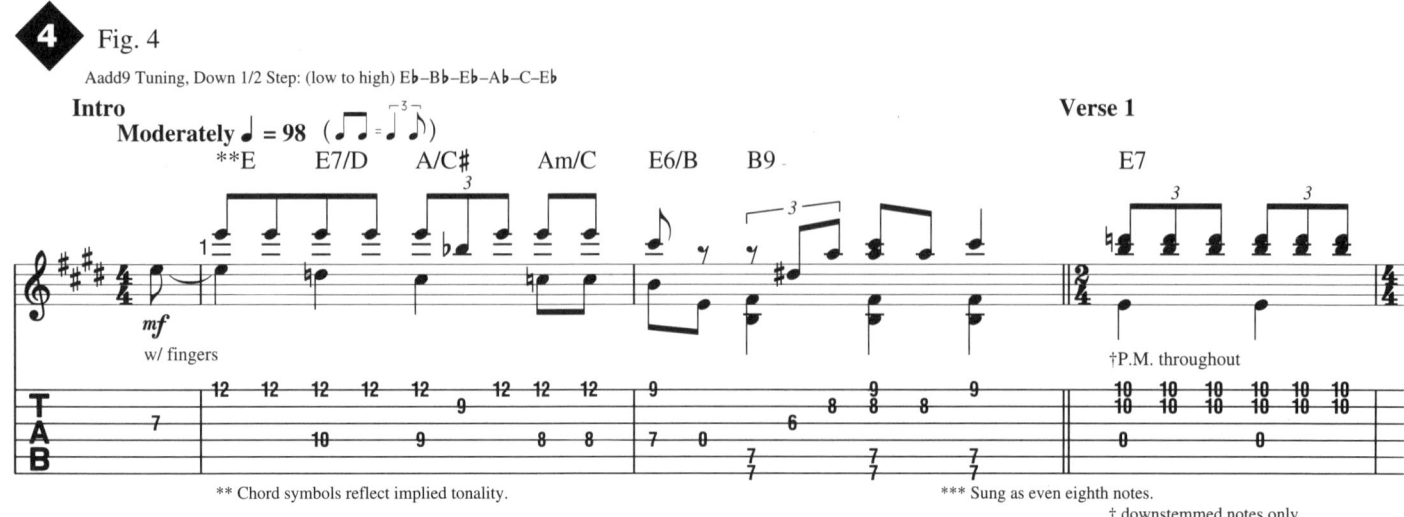

** Chord symbols reflect implied tonality.

*** Sung as even eighth notes.

† downstemmed notes only, except during the turnarounds

Copyright © (1978), 1990, 1991 King Of Spades Music
All Rights Reserved   Used by Permission

SWEET HOME CHICAGO
SA 2582-1

Words and Music by Robert Johnson
(Recorded Monday, November 23, 1936 in San Antonio, Texas)

Fig. 5—Intro and verse 1

Robert Johnson was not the first to *record* a boogie shuffle. That honor goes to Johnny Temple with "Lead Pencil Blues" in 1935. More important than being first is being best, though, and Johnson was so good at this primary blues rhythm that he popularized it beyond his contemporaries.

"Sweet Home Chicago" can be considered the blueprint for all 12-bar boogie shuffles, including Johnson's other variations. The groove is as deep as it gets, with Johnson accenting each down beat with verve to help propel the strutting rhythm.

The two-measure intro with pick up is Johnson's typical descending pattern starting at fret 12. He is not to repeat it until the end of the tune though. He opts instead for a turnaround based on the open position of the E blues scale to close each verse.

Compared to his other material—even the boogie-based numbers—the bass-string boogie patterns accompanying the I and IV chord changes in measures 1-8 are fairly rudimentary. Note that Johnson moves over one set of strings for the IV chord at the same fret position rather than moving a barre up to fret 5 as in "I Believe I'll Dust My Broom." In measure 9 (V), he plays a 2nd inversion chord based on an open position-type fingering usually reserved for the IV chord in his bag of tricks.

Little embellishment takes place except for a classic blues bend in measure 10 of the IV chord. There Johnson holds down the root of the IV chord on string 1 at fret 7 while simultaneously bending the bluesy ♭5th a nifty 1/4 step on string 2. The resulting effect is reminiscent of a train whistle, a sound and image that occupies a special place in the lore of the blues.

Verse 1 and verse 2 share the same arrangement: I chord (1 measure), IV chord (1 measure), I chord (2 measures), IV chord (2 measures), I chord (2 measures), V chord (1 measure), IV chord (1 measure), I chord (1 measure) and V chord (1 measure).

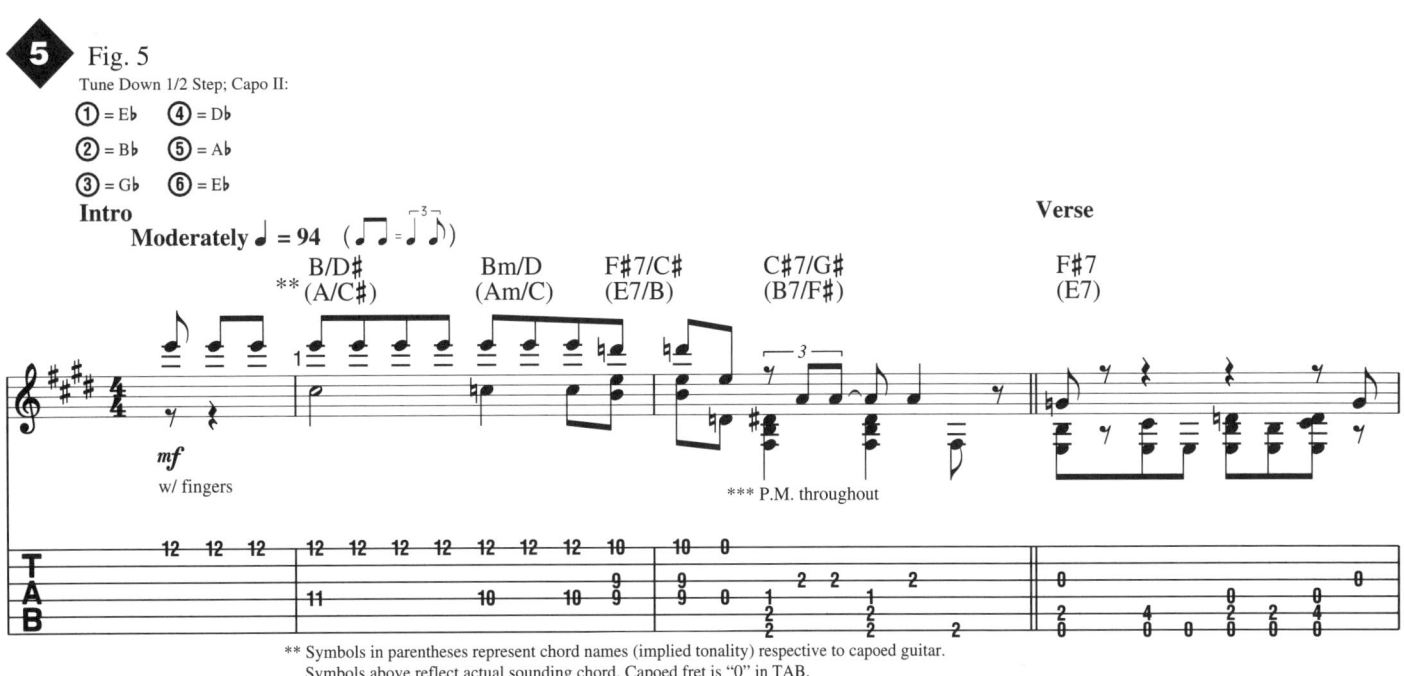

Copyright © (1978), 1990, 1991 King Of Spades Music
All Rights Reserved   Used by Permission

Fig. 6—Verse 3

Verses 3 contains an alternate 12 bar blues arrangement: I chord (4 measures), IV chord (2 measures), I chord (2 measures), V chord (1 measure), IV chord (1 measure), I chord (1 measure) and V chord (1 measure).

RAMBLIN' ON MY MIND

SA 2583-1
Words and Music by Robert Johnson
(Recorded Monday, November 23, 1936 in San Antonio, Texas)

Fig. 7—Intro and Verse 1

Though the "king" of the boogie shufflers and a dangerous slide guitarist, Johnson combined the two elements in only one song, "Ramblin' On My Mind." Interestingly, upon close inspection it is revealed that this composition is the inspiration for the distinctive hook in Elmore James' "Dust My Broom."

The intro is unique as well. Instead of merely starting with a turnaround pattern, Johnson plays a pick up and three measures that mirror the beginning of verse 1, and then tacks on a two-measure turnaround. The pattern used descends in the open position and resolves to the V chord at fret 7. Each of the 5 verses employs this same pattern.

Verse 1 is twelve measures in length. Measures 1-4 contain a *simultaneous* combination of the tonic chord played with the slide at fret 12, and a cut boogie pattern played with the fingers on the open bass strings. You'll have to move fast to add in the 5th on the bass strings while maintaining the aural illusion that you are still vibratoing at fret 12! Measures 5-10 have bass string boogie patterns for the I and IV chords. Note that Johnson plays the V chord boogie pattern in measure 10 on strings 4 and 5 at fret 2, instead of at fret 7. This is an intelligent move on his part as it breaks up the predictability of parallel patterns and it takes advantage of string 5 played open.

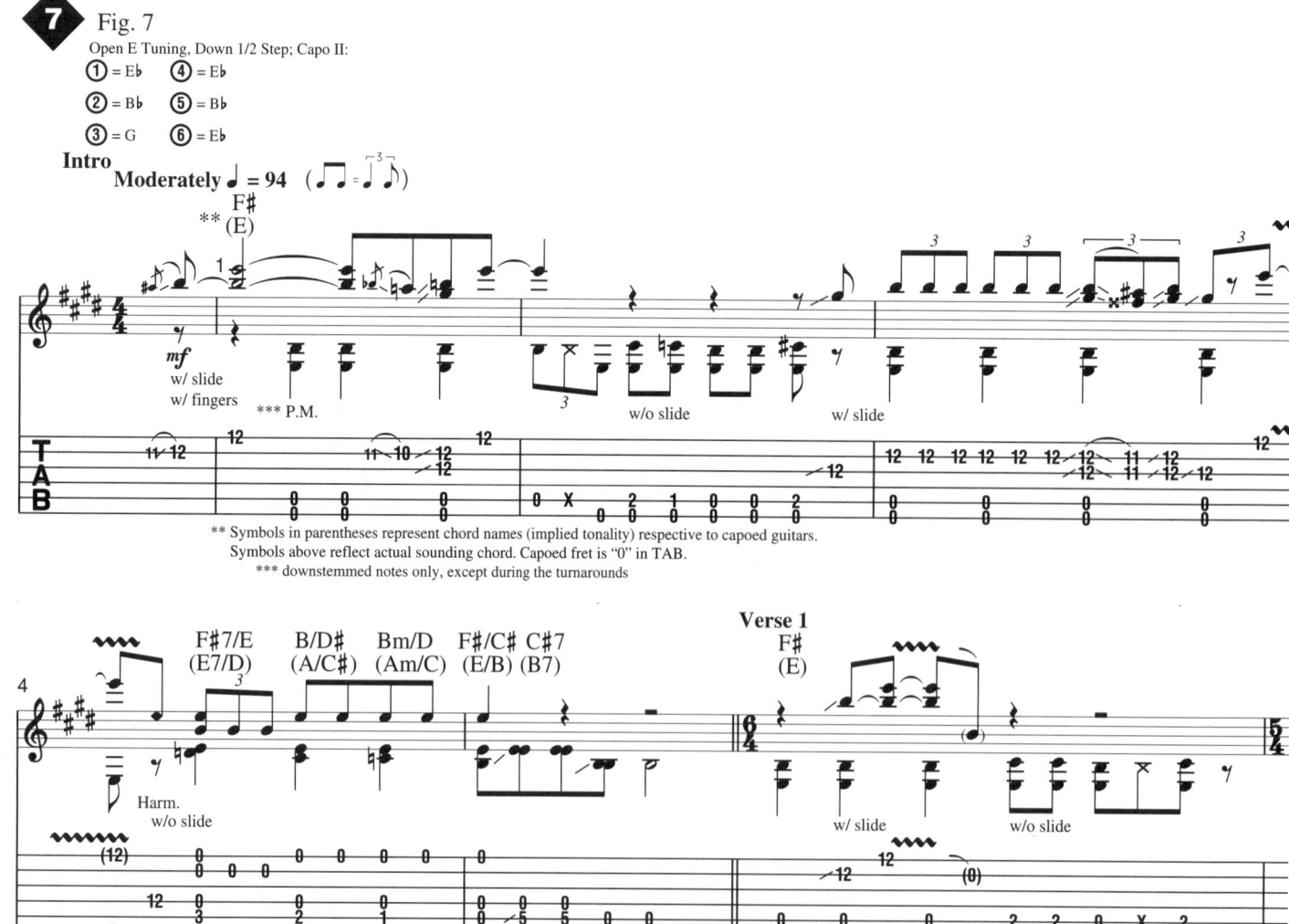

Copyright © (1978), 1990, 1991 King Of Spades Music
All Rights Reserved   Used by Permission

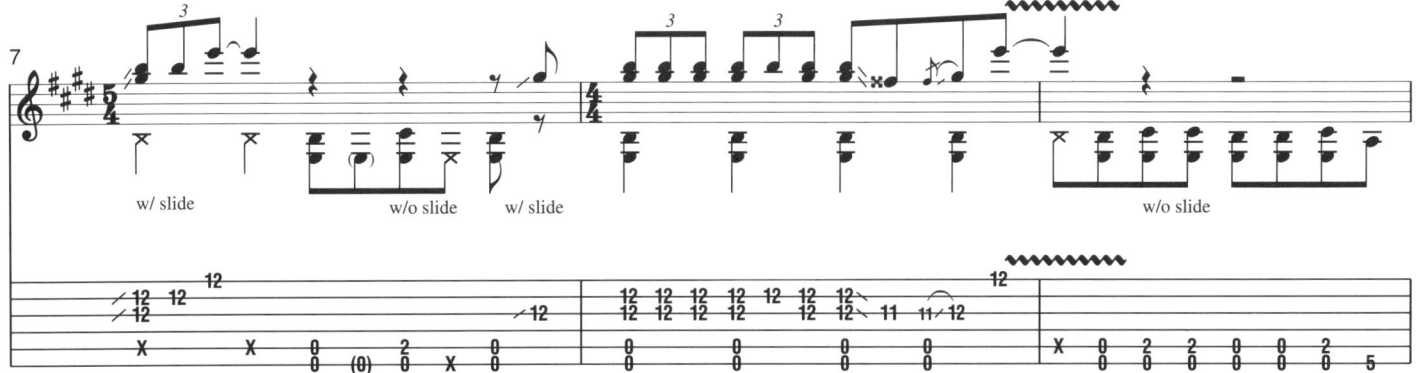

* Tunings were determined using the original 78s. To play along with the *Robert Johnson - The Complete Recordings* CD set, Capo III.

Fig. 8 - Verse 3

Verse 3 is fourteen measures long and begins with a bar of 5/4 time. The extra two measures (5 and 6) are added on to measures 1-4 of the I chord. In measure 6 there's a cool "walk up" (2nd, ♭3rd, and 3rd) in 5ths, from the I to the IV chord on the bass strings.

COME ON IN MY KITCHEN
SA 2585-1
Words and Music by Robert Johnson
(Recorded Monday, November 23, 1936 in San Antonio, Texas)

Fig. 9—Intro and Verse 1

"Come On In My Kitchen" is one of the most profound and moving pieces of music in American history. Singing with the "voice" of a woman, using the word "kitchen" as a sexual metaphor, and caressing the strings with a gentle, delicate touch, Johnson crafted a timeless tale of longing and desire.

The intro consists of three measures with a pick up and contains a "Johnson turnaround" with octaves that resolves to the V chord. As opposed to the vast majority of his recordings, however, this pattern does not appear at the end of each verse.

Verse 1 is 10 measures long and follows the same basic arrangement as the other verses. Johnson wiggles his slider at the octaves (fret 12 in the transcription) while bumping strings 5 and 4 open, creating a "5th" tonality as subtle tension in measures 1-7. The concluding "turnaround" measures then "resolve" to the tonic (I) chord.

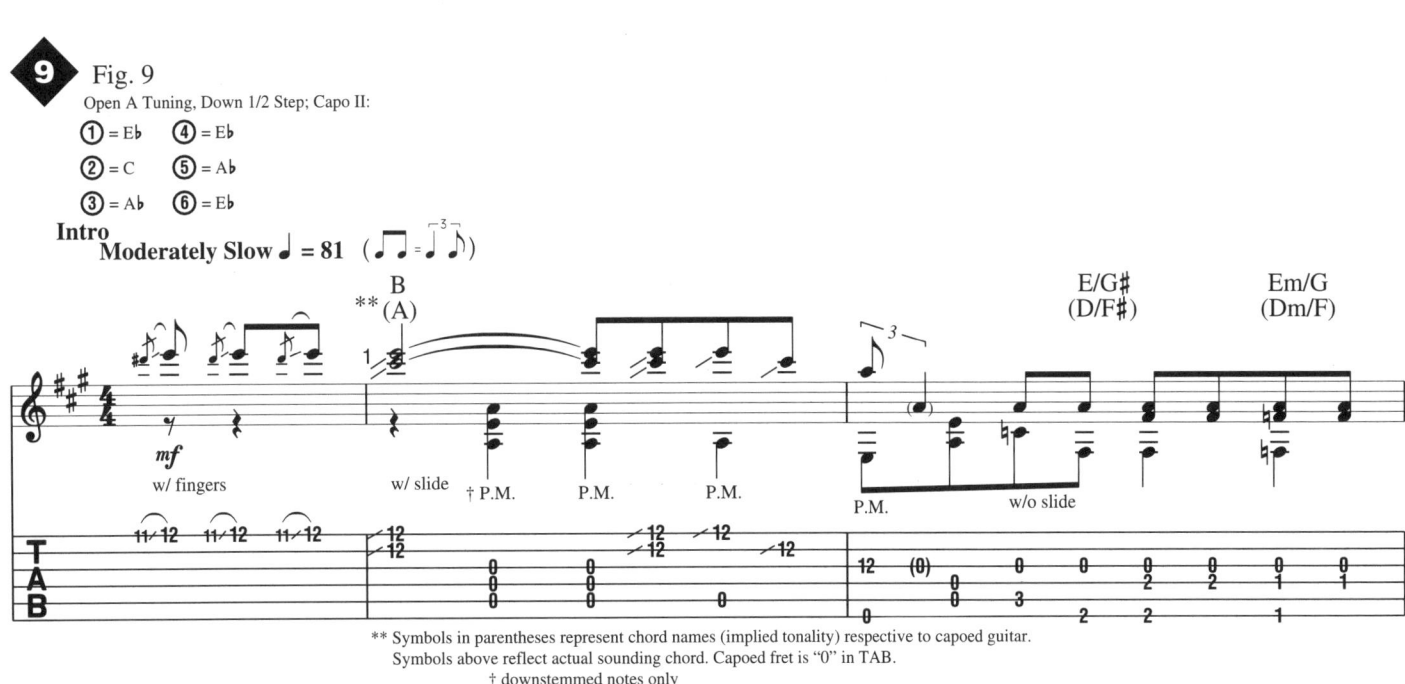

Copyright © (1978), 1990, 1991 King Of Spades Music
All Rights Reserved   Used by Permission

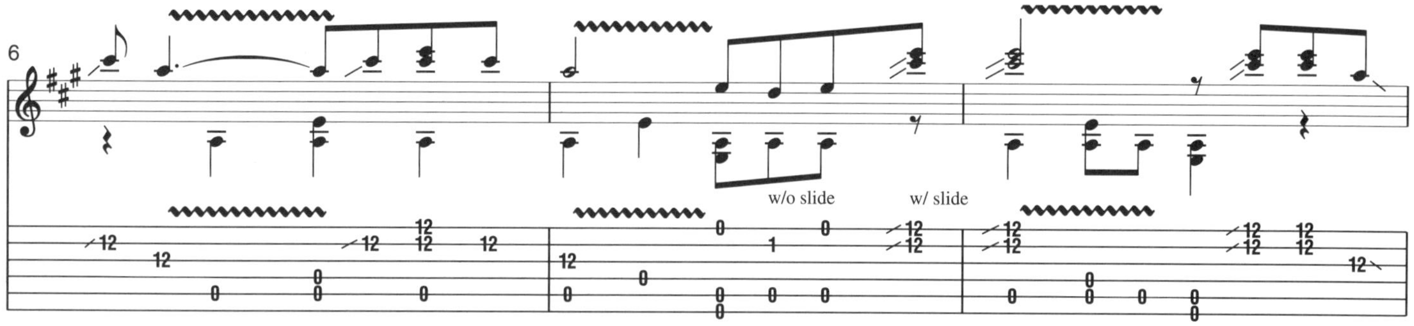

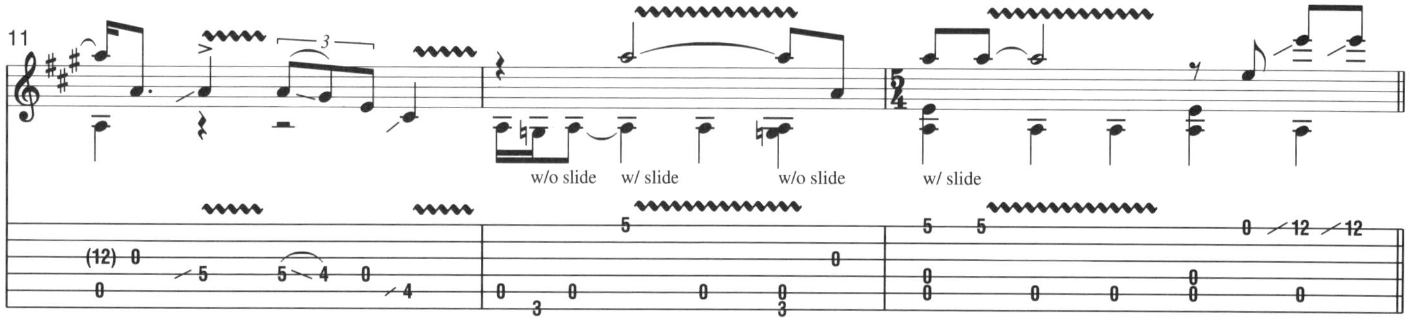

Fig. 10—Verse 3

Verse 3 is only 8 measures long and partially serves as the prologue for the bridge (solo) that follows. Measure 8 (I chord) blends into measure 1 of the bridge.

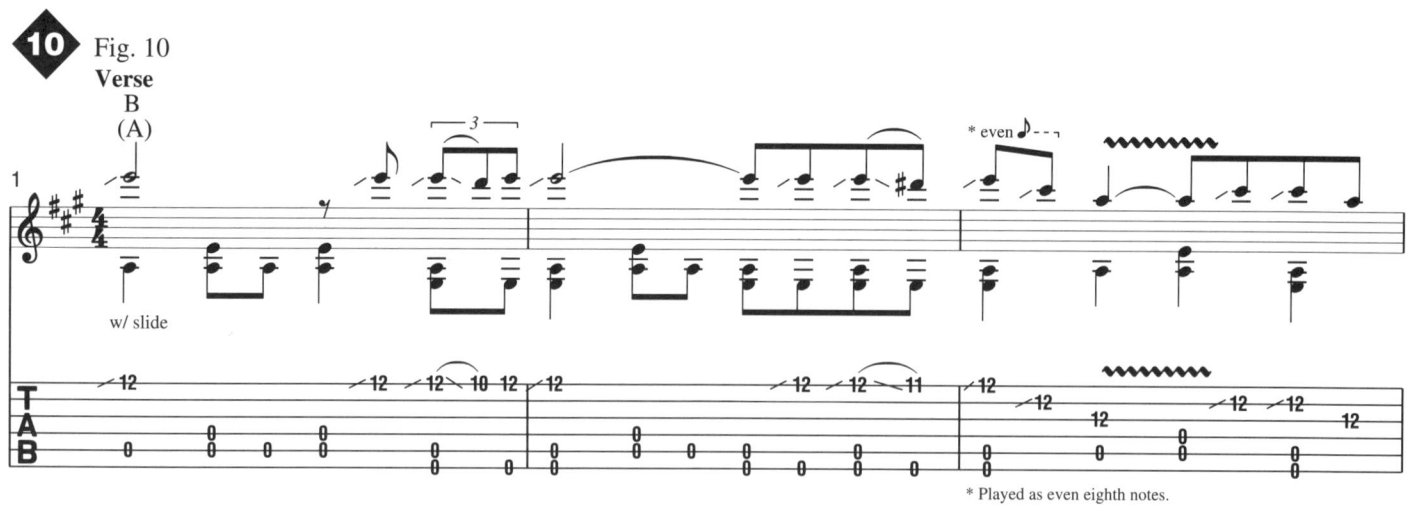

* Played as even eighth notes.

22

Fig. 11—Bridge

The 11-measure bridge functions as a solo even though Johnson does a "voice-over" in measures 1-4. Reaching up above the octave with his bottleneck he performs an uncanny approximation of the wind howling as he asks, "Oh, can't you hear that wind howl?" Measures 5-8 then repeat similar to measures 1-7 in the verses with measures 9-11 as firm resolution to the tonic.

Fig. 12—Verse 5

Verse 5 contains 9 measures, with measures 8 and 9 functioning as the last turn-around.

12 Fig. 12
Verse

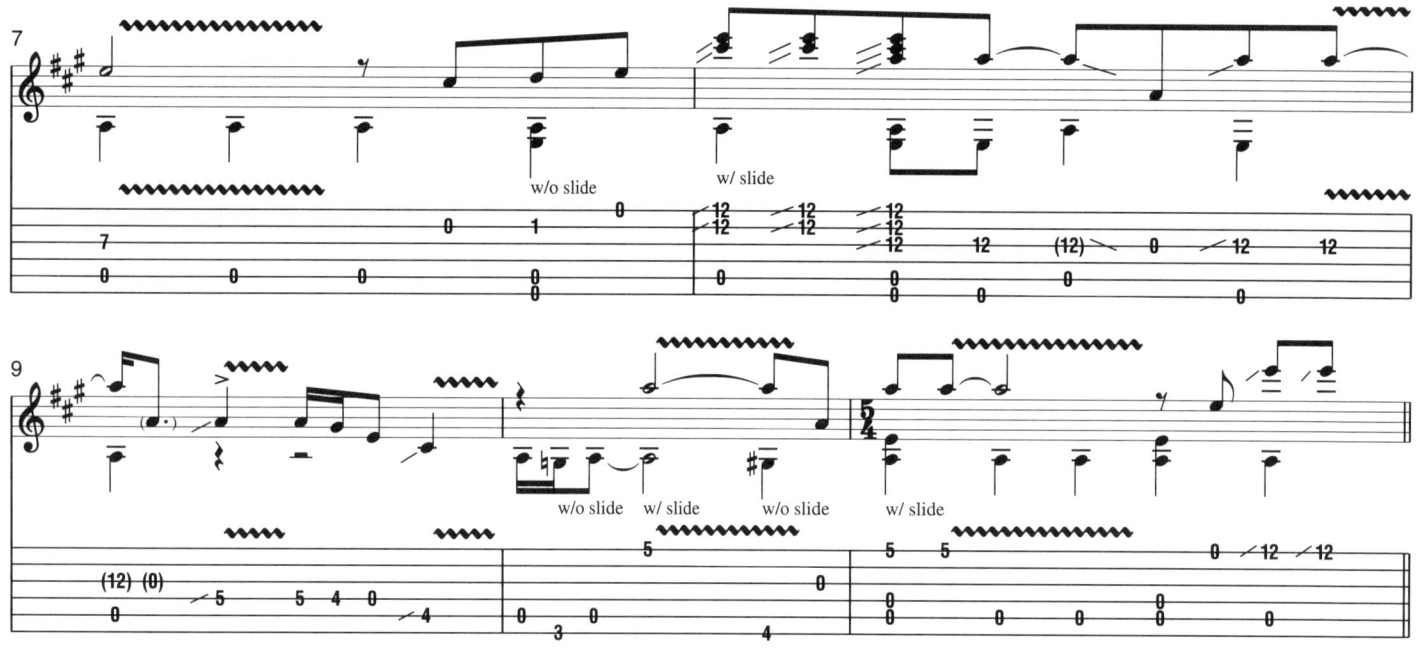

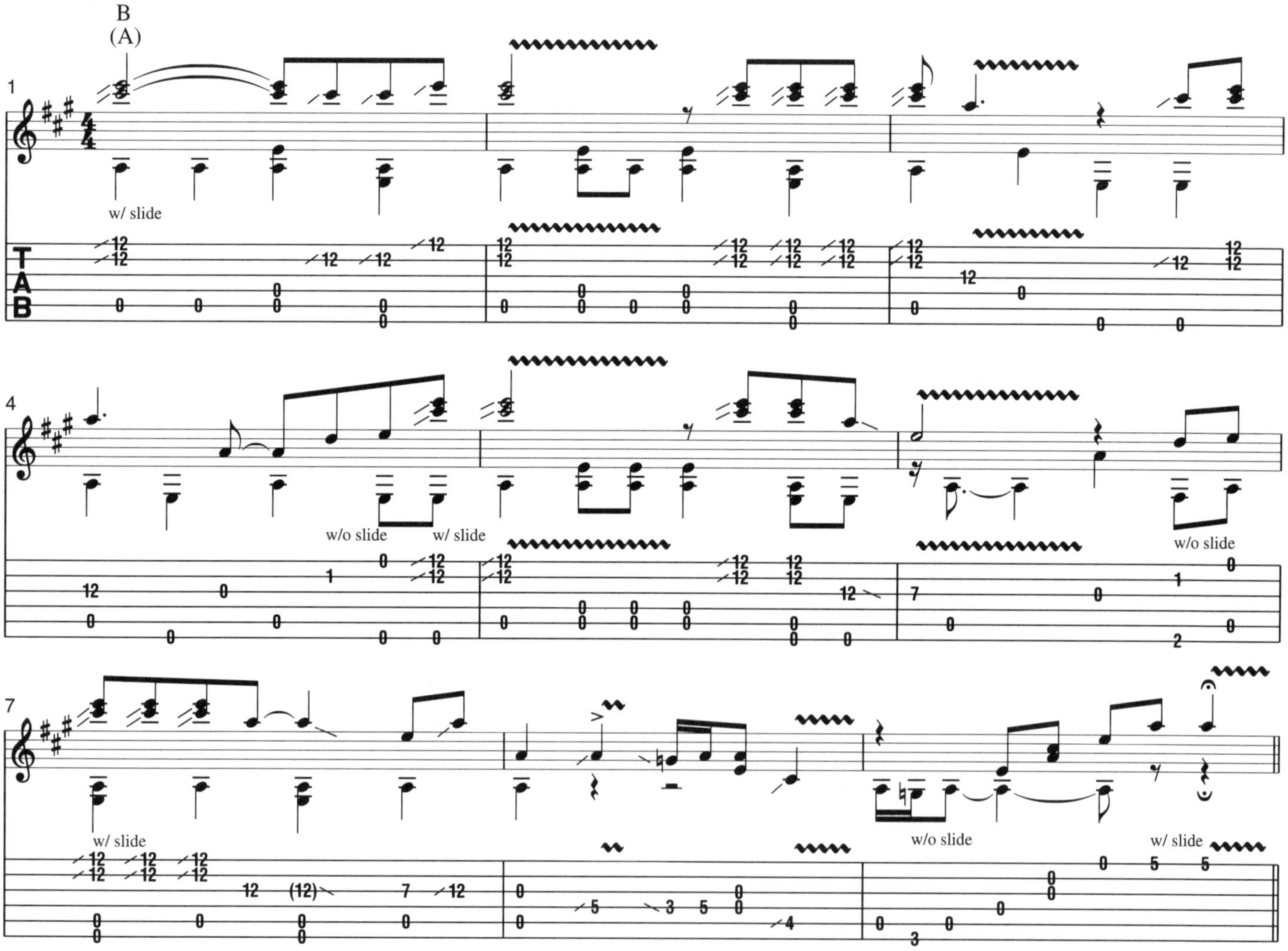

TERRAPLANE BLUES
SA 2586-1
Words and Music by Robert Johnson
(Recorded Monday, November 23, 1936 in San Antonio, Texas)

Fig. 13—Intro and Verse 1

Coupled with "Kind Hearted Woman Blues," "Terraplane Blues" was a modest hit for Johnson in his lifetime. The Terraplane of the title refers ostensibly to a fleet automobile made by Hudson in the thirties. In true blues fashion, of course, it is a convenient sexual metaphor that Johnson "riffs" on throughout the composition. It is also the first recorded example of his "vertical" chord style, with slide and fingers, as opposed to the "linear" style of "Come On In My Kitchen."

The two-measure intro with pick up contains a minimal turnaround that "resolves" to the tonic (I) chord. Like "...Kitchen," it does not repeat at the end of each verse. Verse 1 adheres to the following 12-bar arrangement: I chord = 4 measures, IV chord = 2 measures, I chord = 2 measures, V chord = 1 measure, IV chord = 1 measure and I chord = 2 measures. (Note: Except for the bridge and verse 5, Johnson only applies the slide to *one* note - the root in measure 9 - in each verse. The rest of the time he is fingering dominant chord voicings and licks particular to open A tuning.)

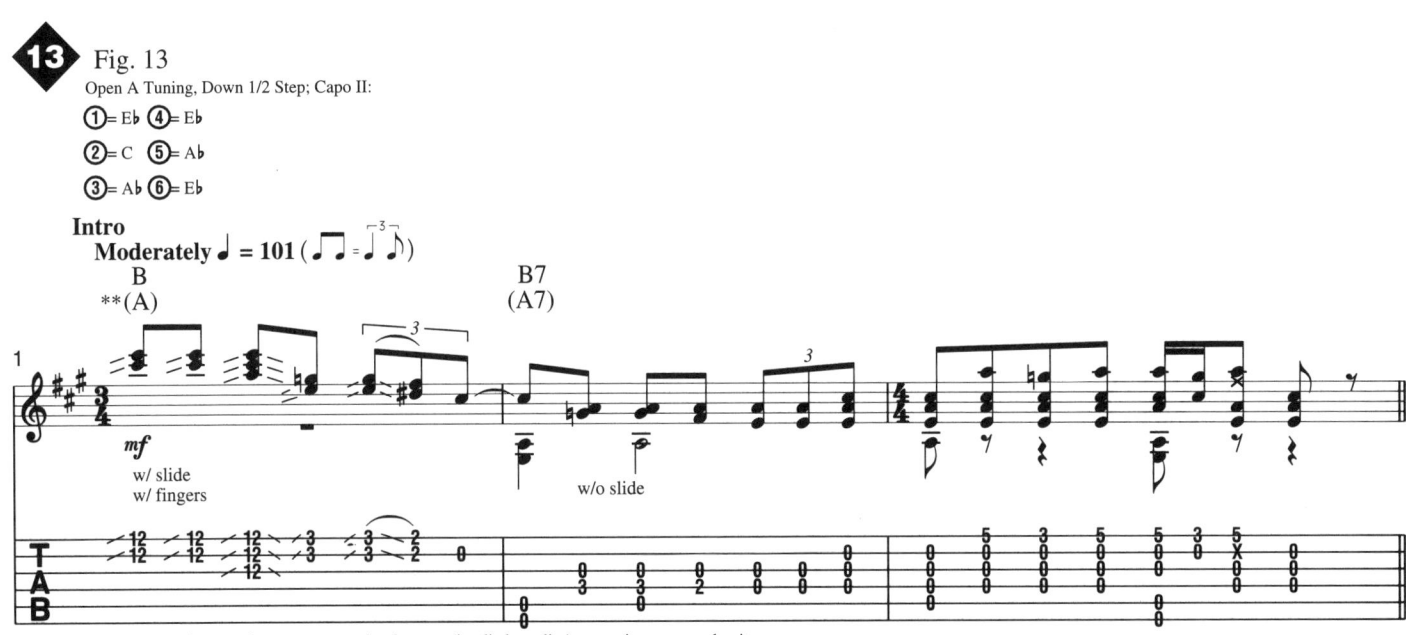

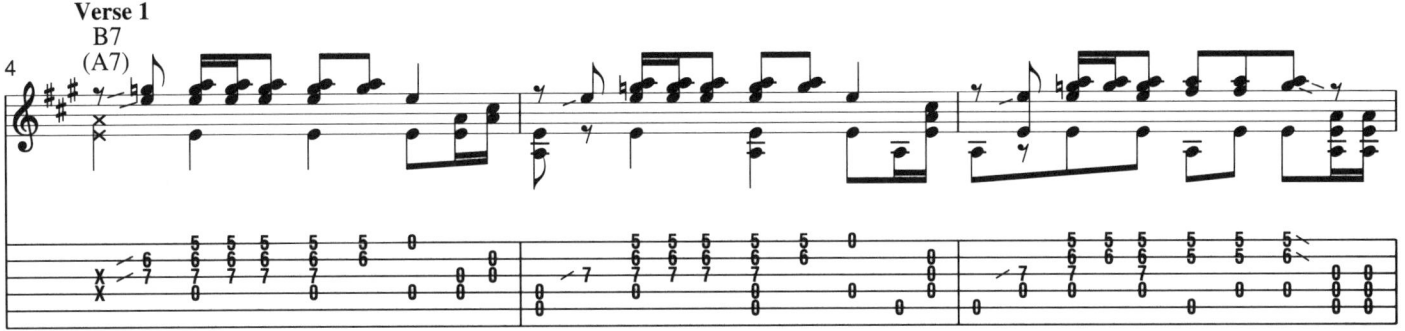

Copyright © (1978), 1990, 1991 King Of Spades Music
All Rights Reserved   Used by Permission

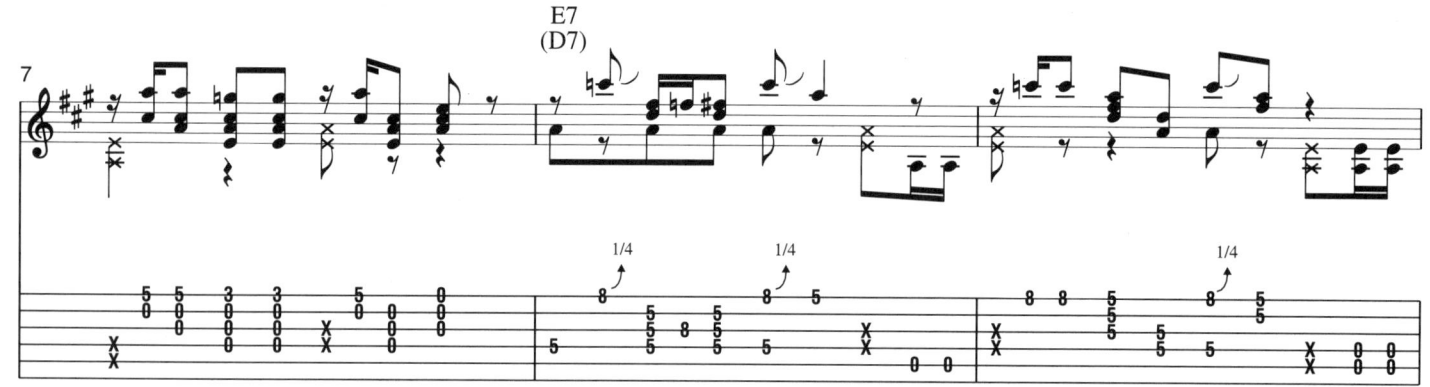
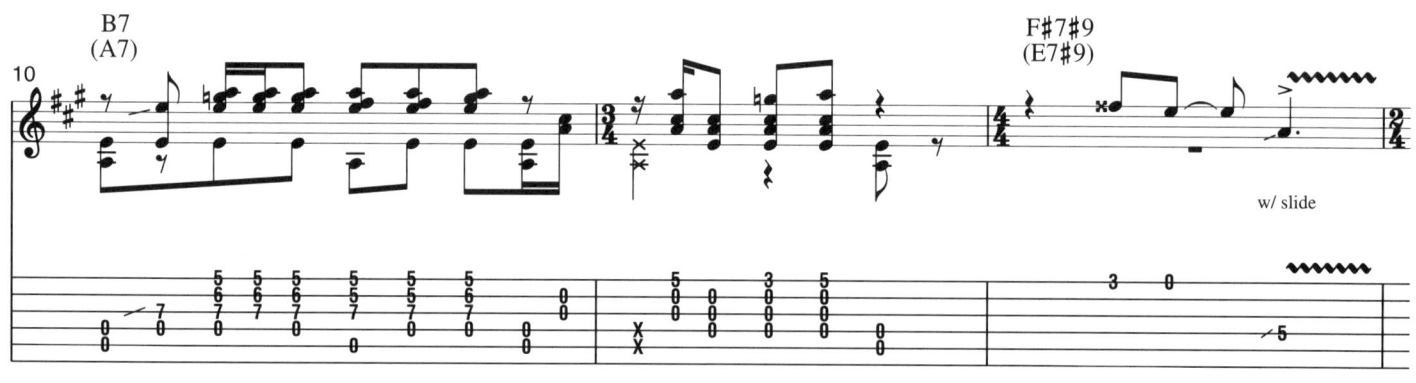
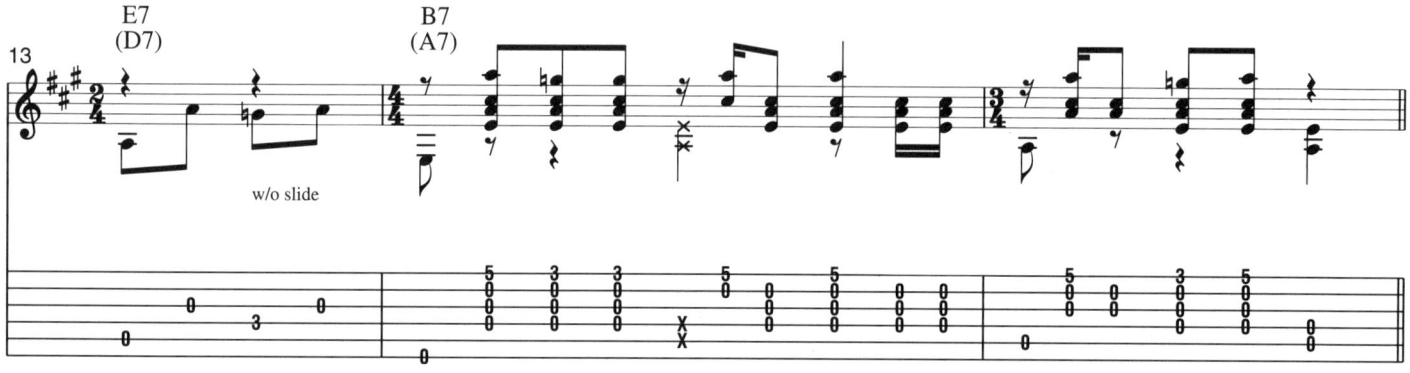

Fig. 14—Bridge

Though 12 measures long like the verses, the bridge introduces a new pattern in measures 1-3 of the I chord. On beat 1 of each measure, Johnson picks the 5th, followed by the I7 voicing and a bass string fill that has since become a staple of blues guitar accompaniment. In addition, in measure 7 he whips the slide up to the octave for a brief flourish similar to the pick up measure in the intro.

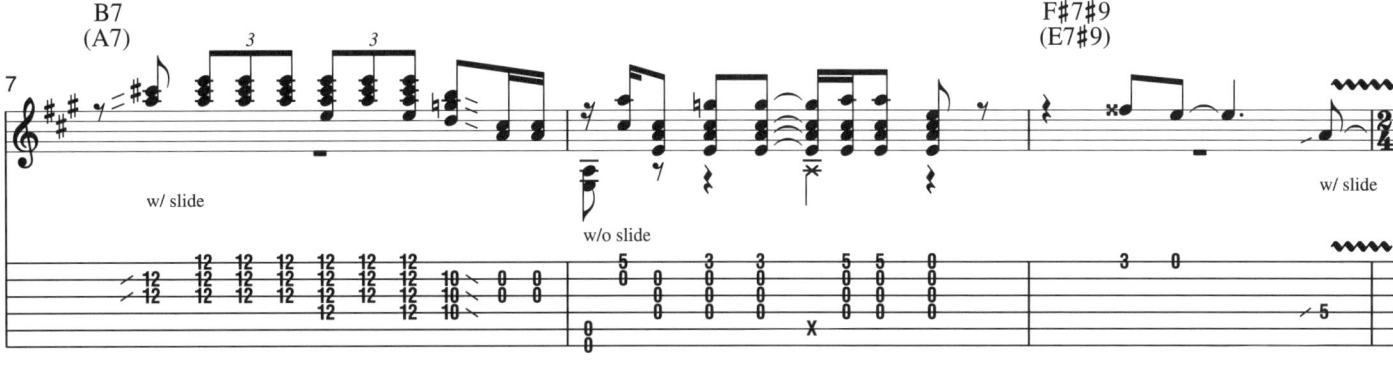

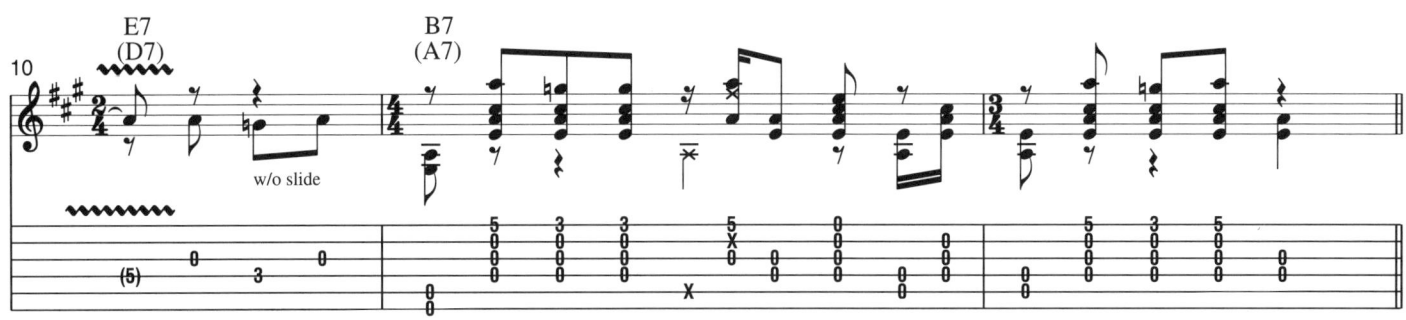

Fig. 15—Verse 4

Verse 4 is virtually the same as the others except that it is 13 measures long, with an extra measure of the I chord tacked on after measure 12.

28

32-20 BLUES
SA 2616-2

Words and Music by Robert Johnson
(Recorded Thursday, November 26, 1936 in San Antonio, Texas)

Fig. 16—Intro and Verse 1

After a two-day layoff, Johnson came back on Thursday to record this one selection. It is open to speculation as to why this occurred, but Johnson biographer Steve LaVere believes that the period between the two sessions may have been when the San Antonio police allegedly beat up Johnson. It is a plausible explanation of why he was only up for one track and why he seems to be a little nervous in his performance, as powerful as it is, as he adds and drops beats. Like "Walkin' Blues," "32-20" has a steady quarter-note pulse underneath that suggests an independent bass accompaniment.

The 4-measure intro with pick up contains the "double turnaround" beginning with the I7 triple stop that Johnson popularized. Notice that measures 3 and 4 of the intro are the basis for the turnarounds at the end of each verse.

Verse 1 is 13 measures long with an extra measure of the I chord in 2/4 time in measure 4. The main I-IV theme is played around fret 5 with I7 and I°7 implied with a minimal number of notes. Check out that Johnson "nervously" goes to the diminished chord for a second time in measure 4, something that he does not do anywhere else in "32-20" nor in any of his other songs.

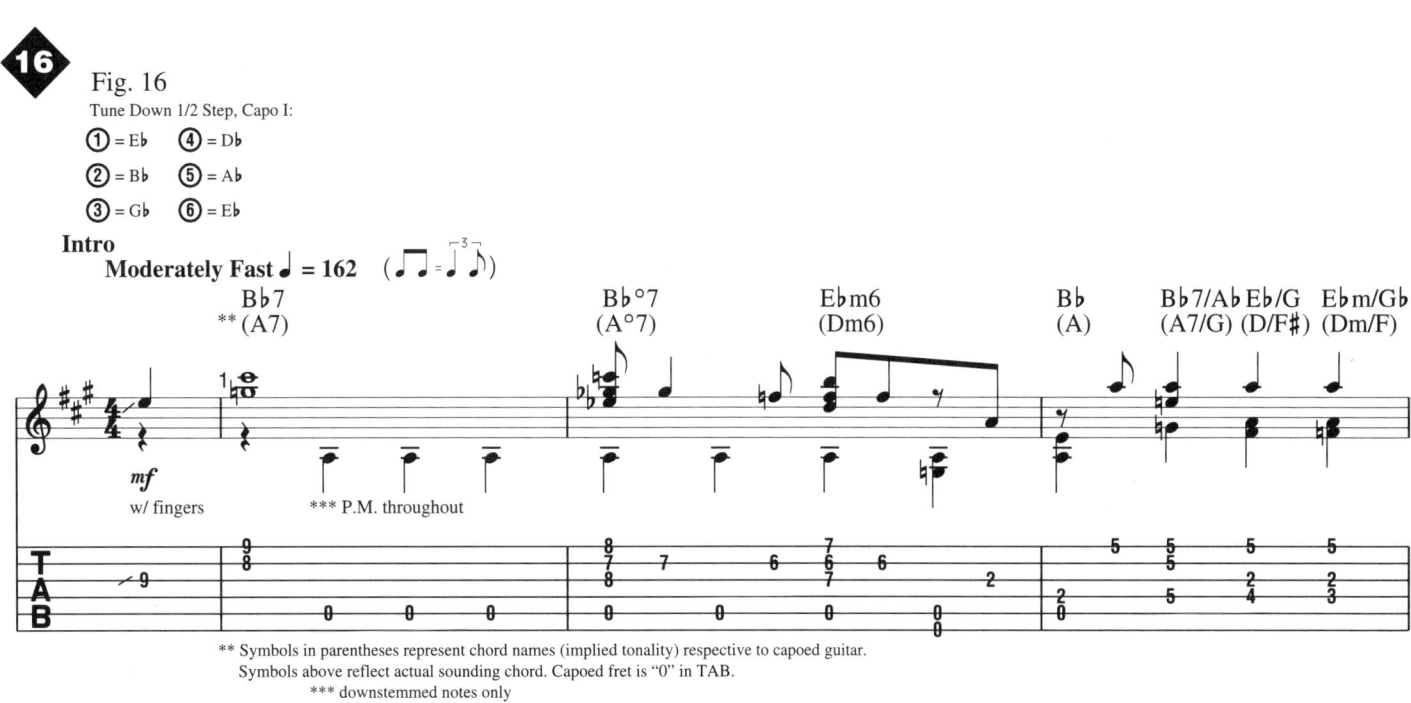

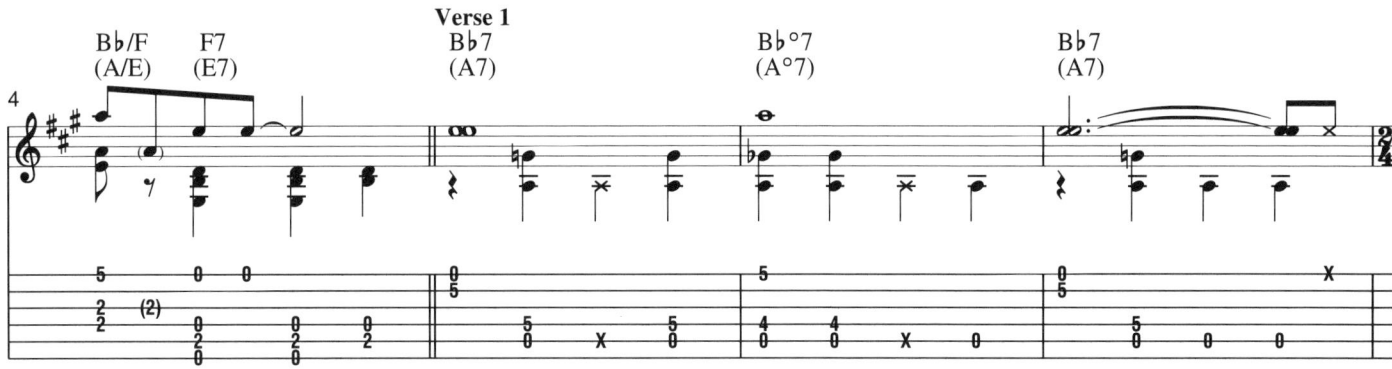

Copyright © (1978), 1990, 1991 King Of Spades Music
All Rights Reserved   Used by Permission

Fig. 17—Verse 2

Verse 2 begins with the dominant triple stop from the intro, then moves it down the fingerboard one fret to indicate the change to the I°7 chord in measure 2 of the 12-bar progression. Notice the descending I chord pattern, based around the barre chord at fret 2, that appears in measures 4 and 8. It appears in all of the verses with slight phrasing variation and functions as a secondary theme.

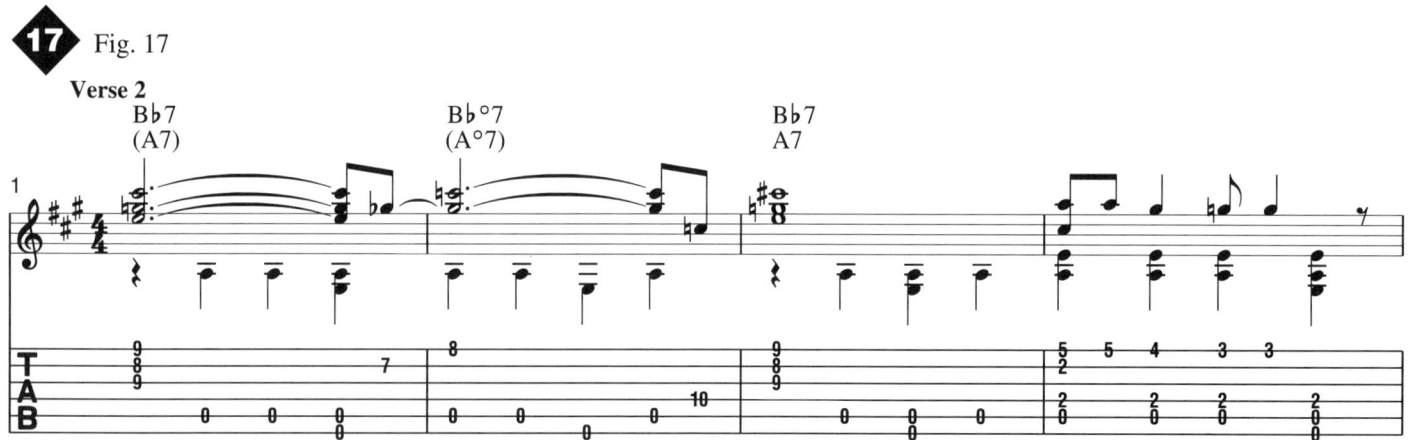

Fig. 18—Verse 6

Verse 6 shows Johnson altering the dominant triple-stop in measure 1 from Fig. 17, to become a 2nd inversion major triad. Instead of moving the entire form down one fret as in previous verses, however, he maintains the position of the note on string 2 (root) while lowering the note on string one (3rd). When combined with string 3 open (b7th), it implies a im7 chord rather than a I°7 chord. Compare this to verse 10 (Figure 19), the last verse of "32-20," where Johnson takes the same 2nd inversion triad and moves it intact down one fret. Now the result is to create a major triad 1/2 step lower than the tonic chord. Did Johnson consciously plan all this? Probably, because he also alters his right hand technique, swinging the chords in measures 1-3 of verse 6 and 10 like a big band guitarist, while eschewing the quarter-note bass accompaniment.

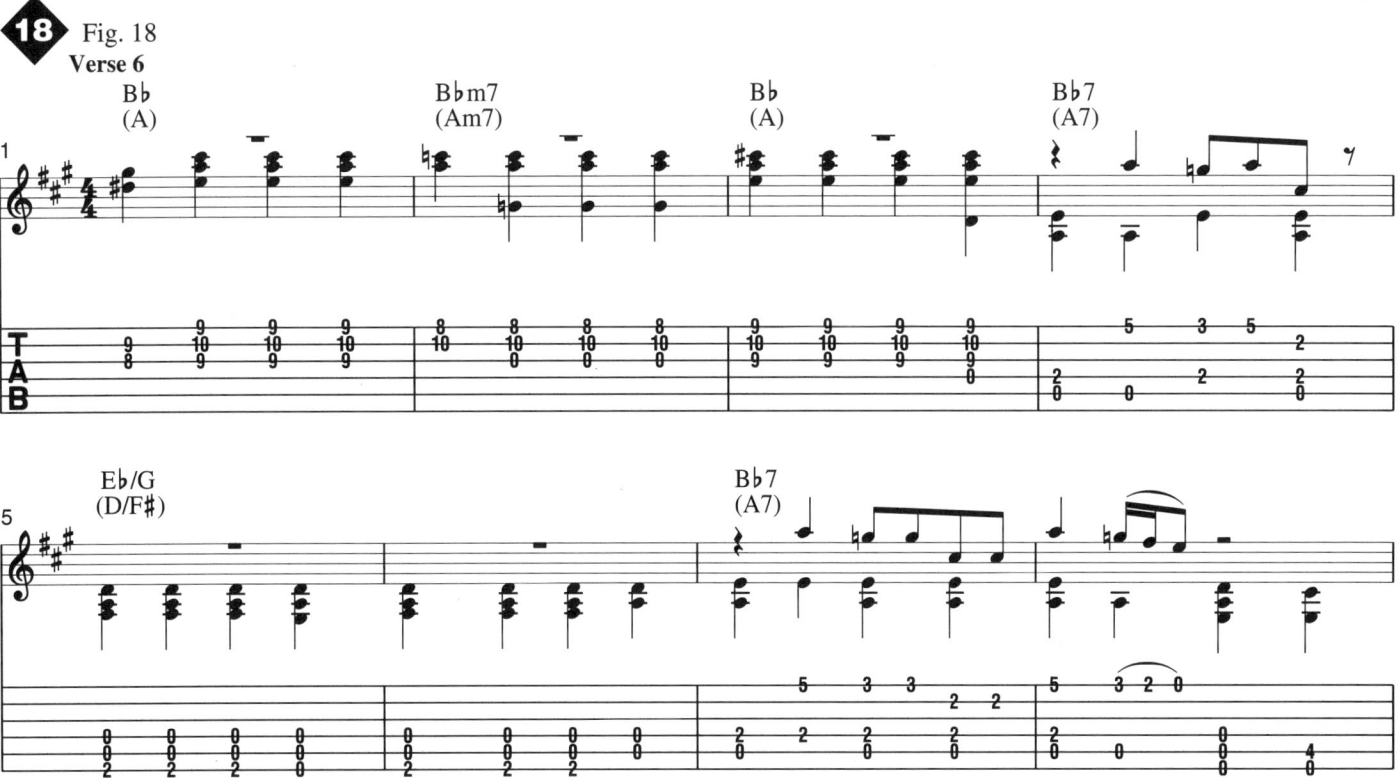

Fig. 19—Verse 10

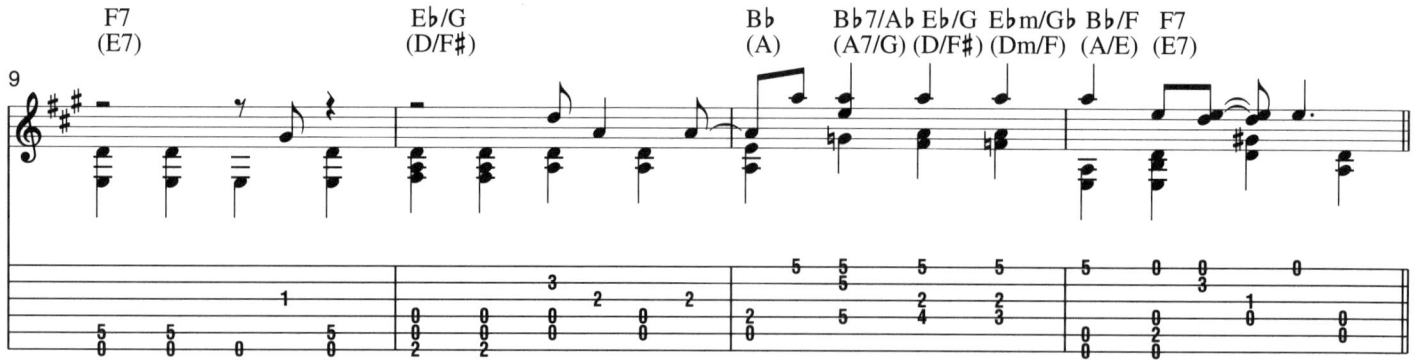

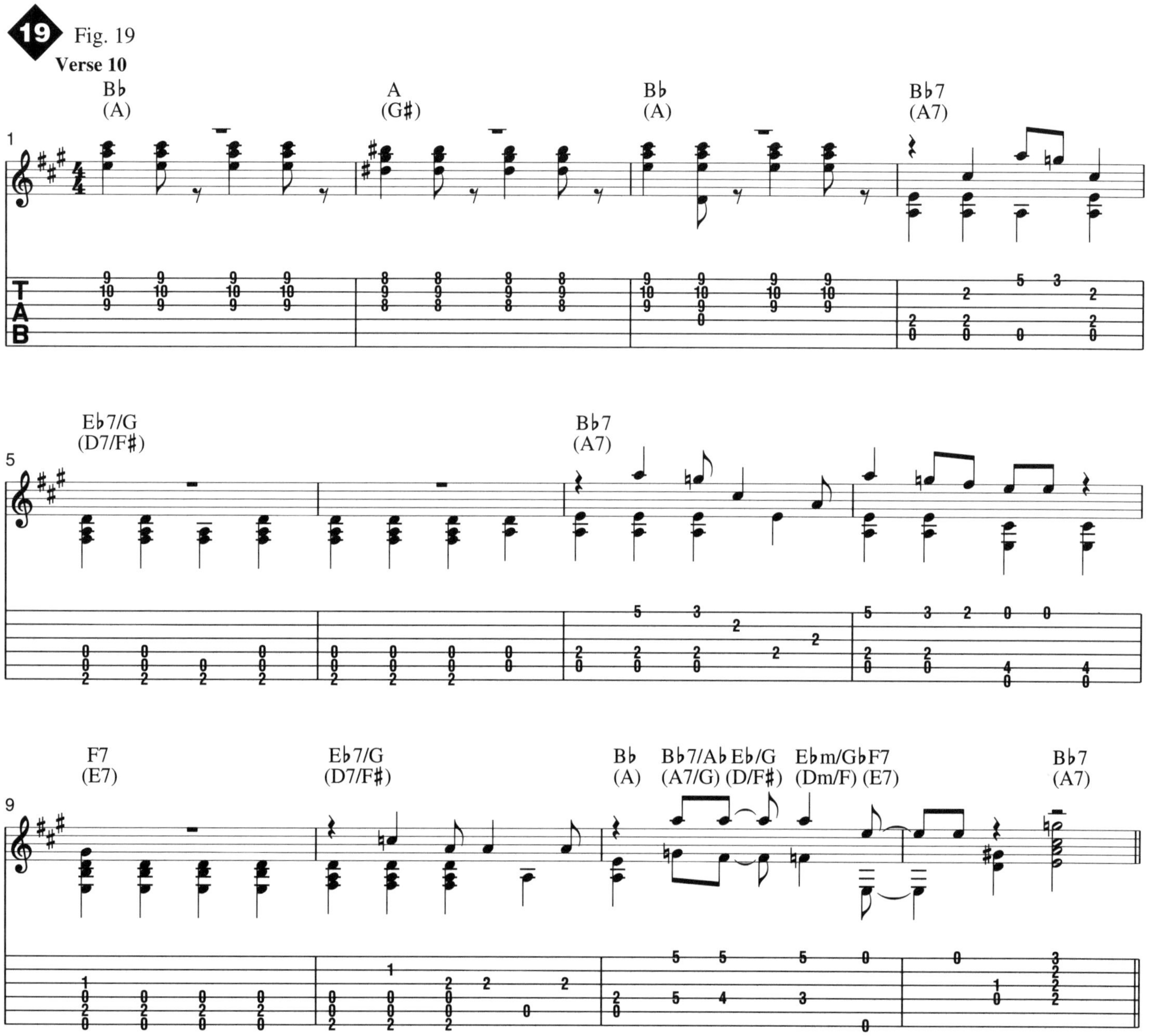

CROSS ROAD BLUES (CROSSROADS)
SA 2629-2
Words and Music by Robert Johnson
(Recorded Friday, November 27, 1936 in San Antonio, Texas)

Fig. 20—Intro and Verse 1

"Cross Road Blues" is one of Johnson's major contributions to the musical language of blues guitar via the rich chordal harmony played throughout with the slide. The next step in the development of concepts first introduced in "Terraplane Blues," it's aggressive, syncopated rhythms and combination of fretted notes and slide make it a challenge for the guitarist and a profound experience for the listener. Unfortunately, a certain amount of notoriety has become attached to the piece thanks to the overheated imagination of blues writers in the mid-sixties and Eric Clapton's galvanic 1968 version with Cream. Both events were the source for the "selling the soul at the cross roads" myth. (See *The Road to Robert Johnson* by Edward Komara, published by the Hal Leonard Corporation, for a detailed discussion of this phenomenon.)

"Cross Road Blues" is based on an "expanded" 12-bar blues progression with verses of 15 and 14 measures. Figure 20 shows the 4-measure intro and verse 1. The intro starts with two measures of slide that begin at the octave and resolve to the root at fret 5. Measures 3 and 4 have a descending turnaround pattern particular to open A tuning, played with the fingers and resolving to the 5th. Note that this pattern does not function for the turnarounds at the end of each verse, and that in fact, there are no turnarounds in the song.

Verse 1 contains 15 measures in the following arrangement: I (6 measures), IV (2 measures), I (3 measures), V (1 measure), and I (3 measures). Check out that measures 9-11 of the I chord are the same as measures 13-15. Also, see that the I chord change always consists of a combination of slide and fretted notes while the IV and V chords contain fretted licks only.

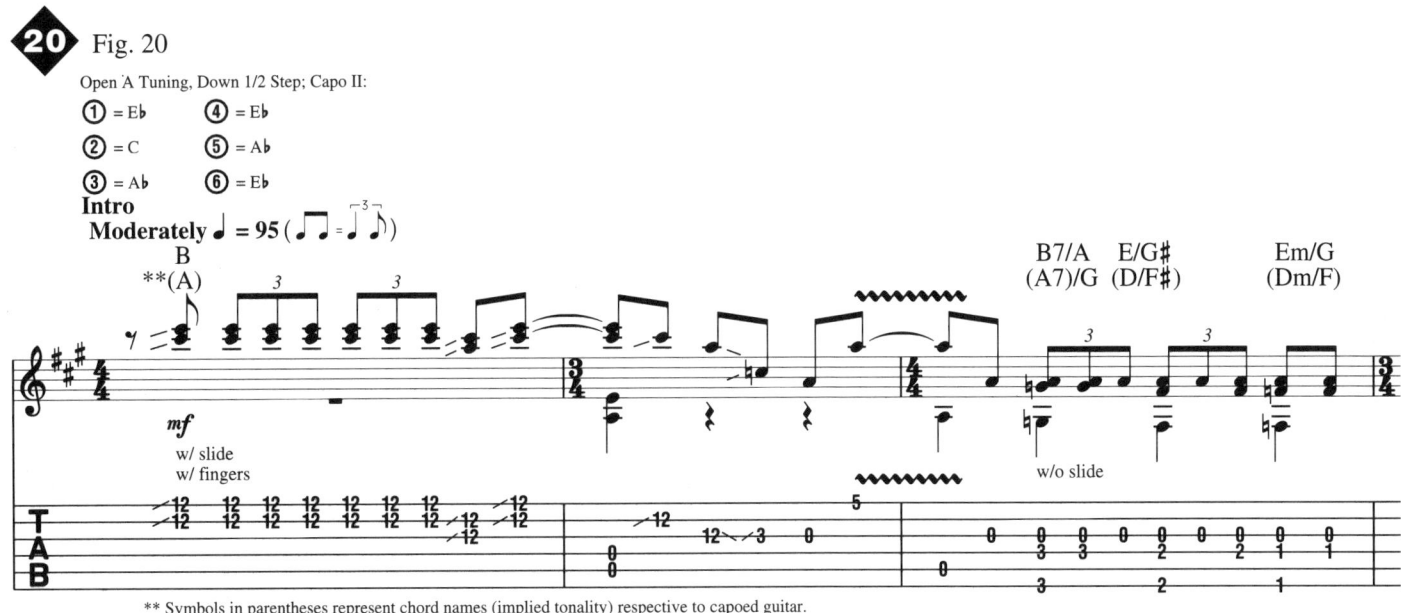

** Symbols in parentheses represent chord names (implied tonality) respective to capoed guitar.
Symbols above reflect actual sounding chord. Capoed fret is "0" in TAB.

Copyright © (1978), 1990, 1991 King Of Spades Music
All Rights Reserved   Used by Permission

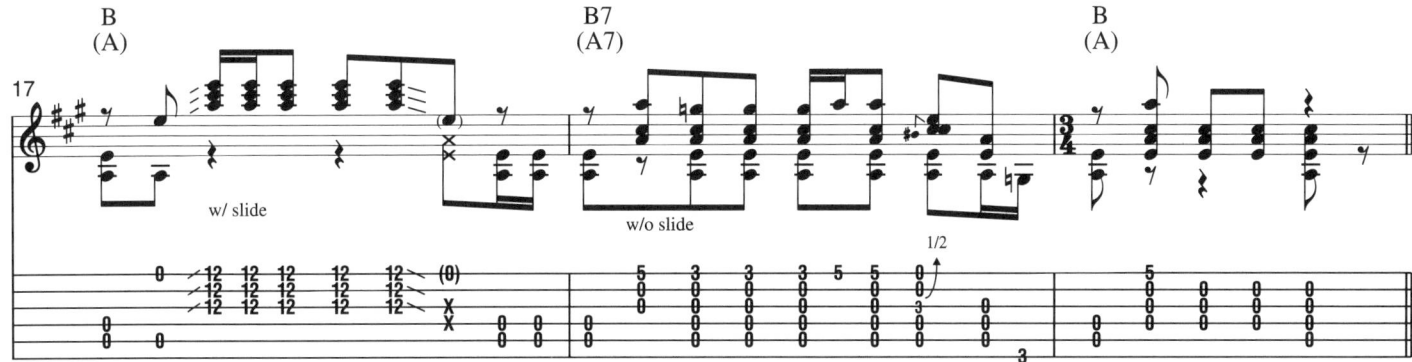

Fig. 21—Verse 2

Verse 2 is 14 measures long in the following arrangement: I (5 measures), IV (2 measures), I (3 measures), V (I measure), and I (3 measures). The forms are similar to verse 1 except for the V chord (measure 11) which has a sparse, single-note line of slide notes, and measure 12 of the I chord that has a fretted bass-string pattern instead of the octave lick with the slide. Both changes add dynamics when contrasted with the chordal forms prevalent throughout.

21 Fig. 21

Verse 2

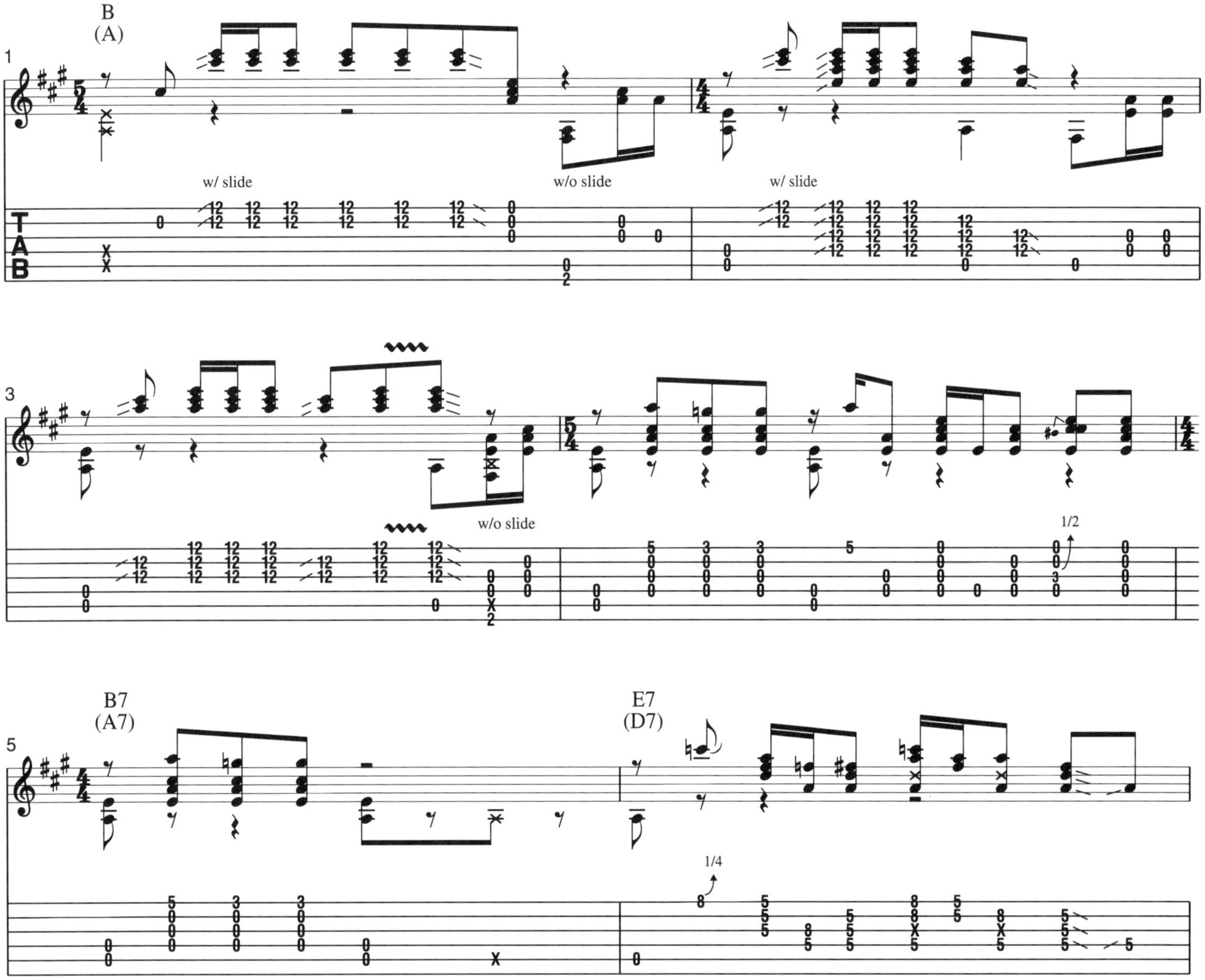

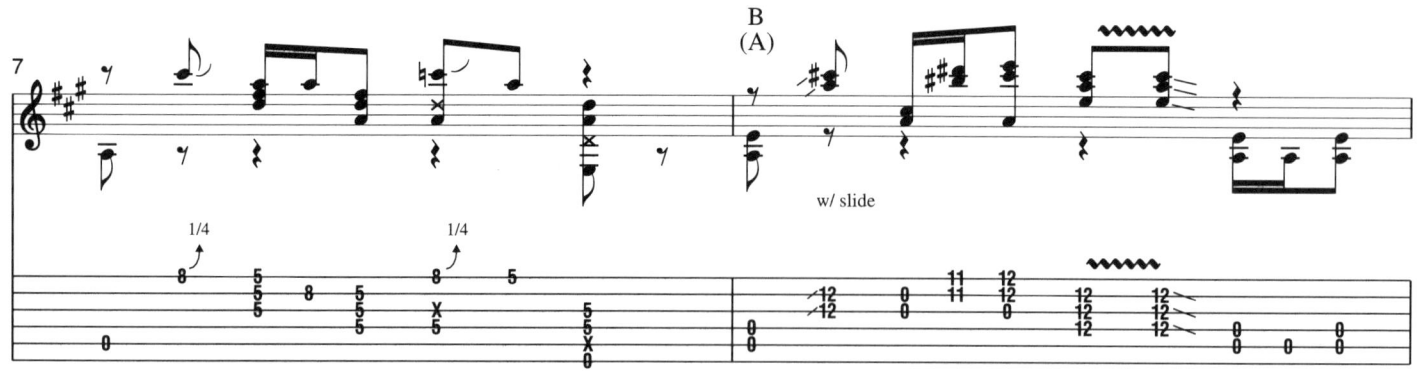

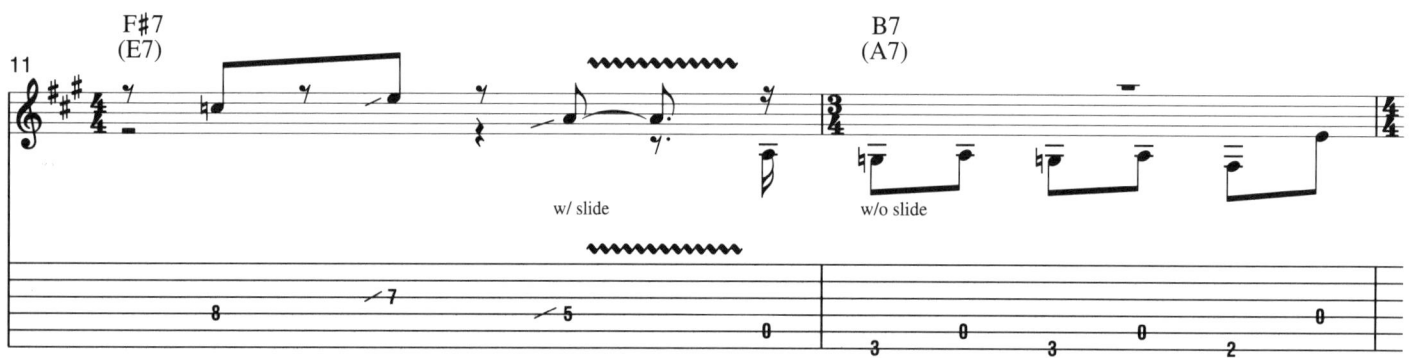
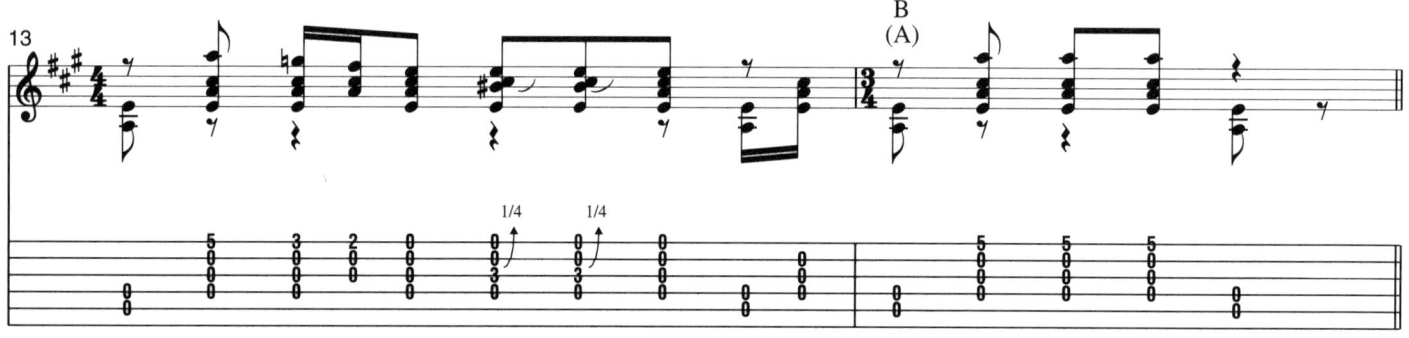

Fig. 22—Verse 3

Verse 3 has the same arrangement as verse 2. Where it differs is in measure 11 (V chord) and measure 12 (I chord). For the V chord (an implied 7#9) Johnson leaves plenty of musical space while suggesting the chord with two fretted notes on the treble strings and a succinct bass fill. As he did in verse 1, he returns to the octave with his slider for the I chord before continuing with fretted notes at the 5th position in measures 13 and 14.

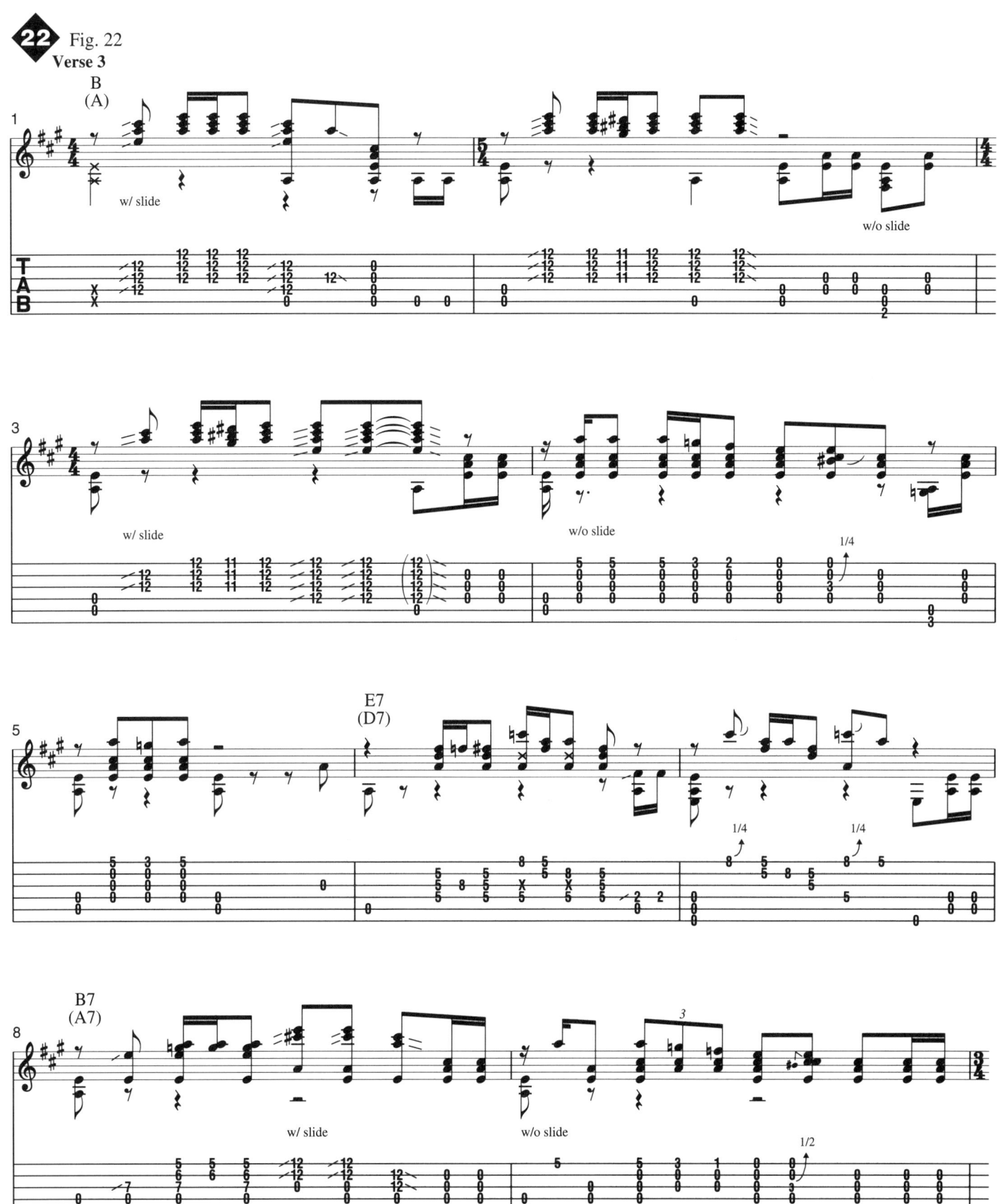

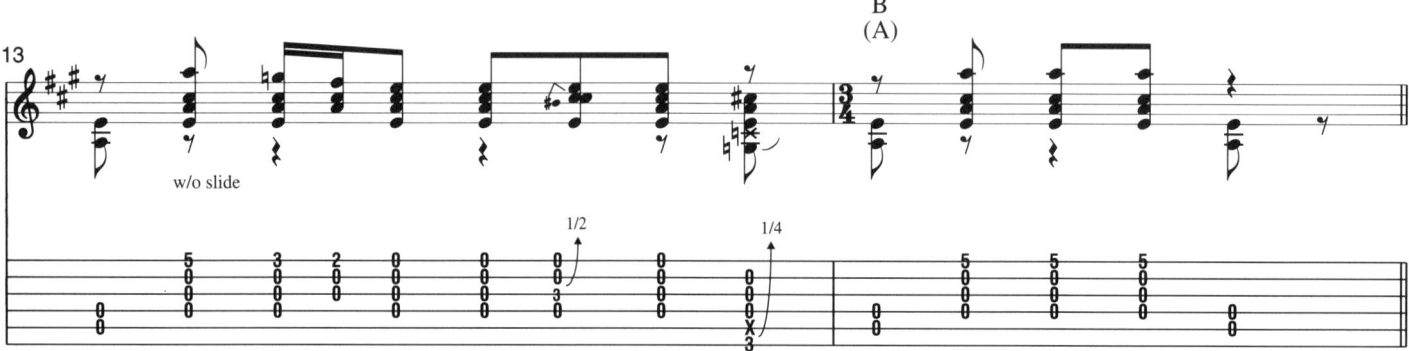

Fig. 23—Verse 4

Verse 4 is 15 measures in length like verse 1. The extra measure occurs at the end of the tune, however, so that the arrangement is similar in all ways to verse 2 except for the added measure of the I chord.

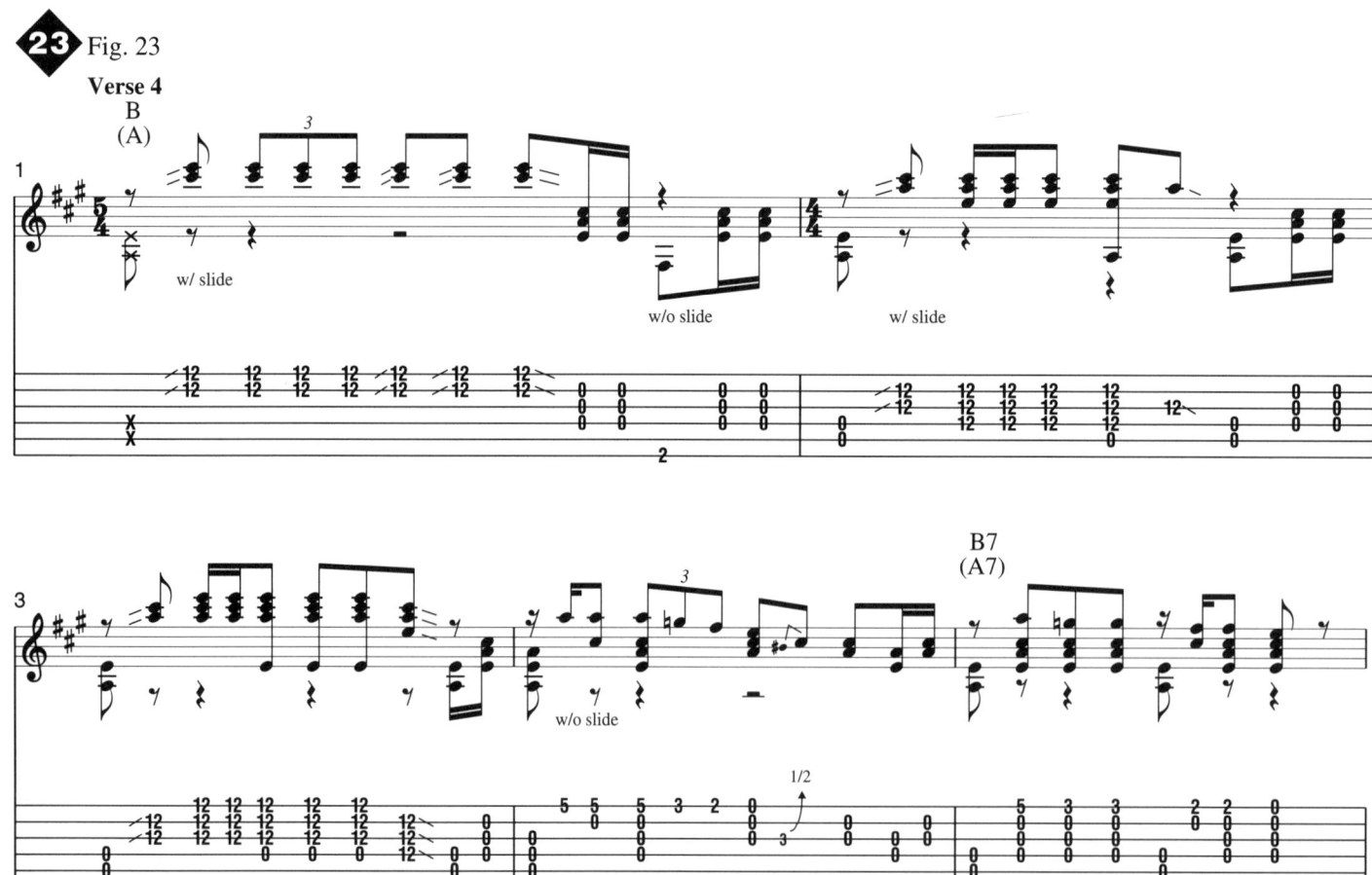

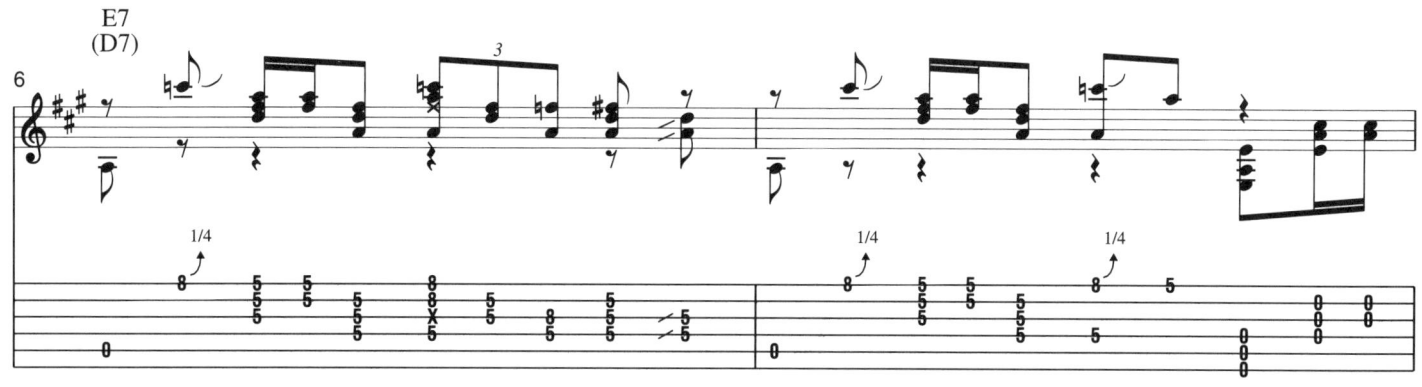
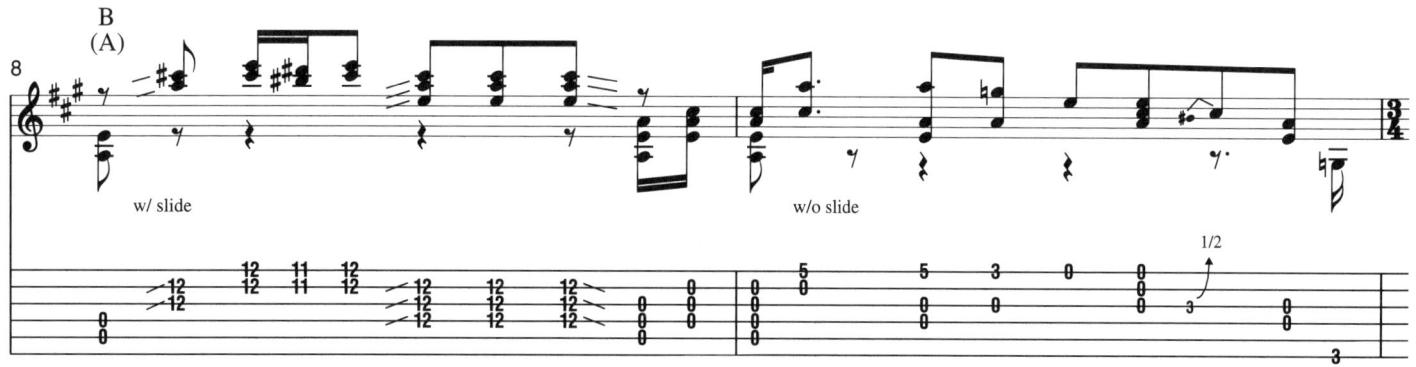
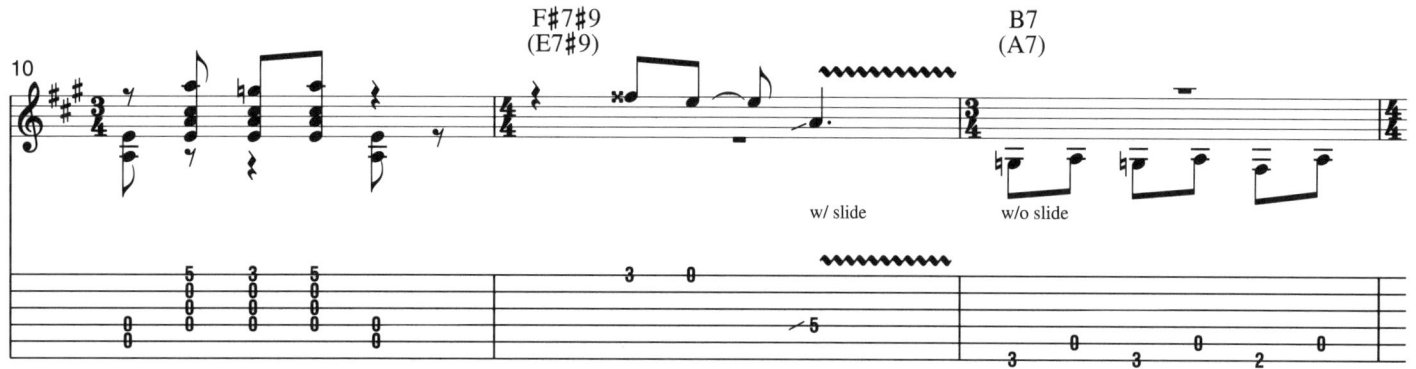
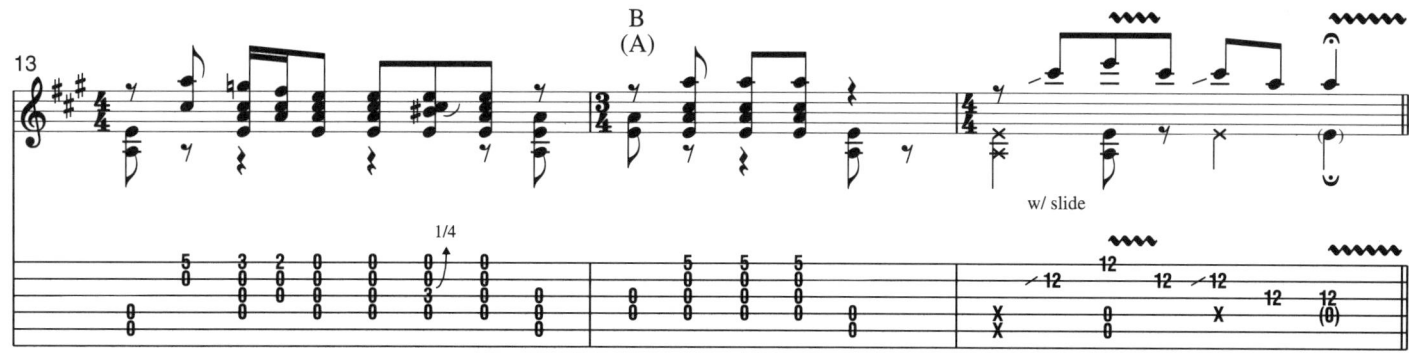

WALKIN' BLUES
SA 2630-1
Words and Music by Robert Johnson
(Recorded Friday, November 27, 1936 in San Antonio, Texas)

Fig. 24—Intro and verse 1

Though clearly based on the Son House composition, "My Black Mama," Johnson's "Walkin' Blues" is a superior number in every way. In the tradition of work songs known as "ax-falls," which refers to field hands timing their ax swings to fall on the first beat of each measure of a song chosen to synchronize the task, it showcase's Johnson's deep blues groove, rhythmic independence and slide intonation.

The 3-measure intro is similar to "Cross Road Blues" inasmuch as it begins with Johnson's typical double-stop slide lick on the top two strings at the octave, followed by the 2-measure, fretted, descending turnaround pattern in open A. Again, like the previous tune, this sequence does not appear at the end of the verses, as they contain no turnaround.

Verses 1 and 2 employ the following arrangement: I chord (4 measures), IV chord (2 measures), I chord (2 measures), IV chord (1 measure), V chord (1/2 measure), IV chord (1/2 measure), and I chord (2 measures). All of the I chord measures consist of plucked open strings and slide embellishments on strings 5 and 1. The IV chord in measures 5 and 6 is based around the root note on string 5 played with the slide, and a bass string fill leading back to the I chord. The IV-V-IV changes in measures 9 and 10 are similarly phrased. Be aware that it is of paramount importance to angle the slide up and away from all the strings except string 1 in order to avoid interfering with fretted notes and open strings for the bass part of the arrangement throughout the song.

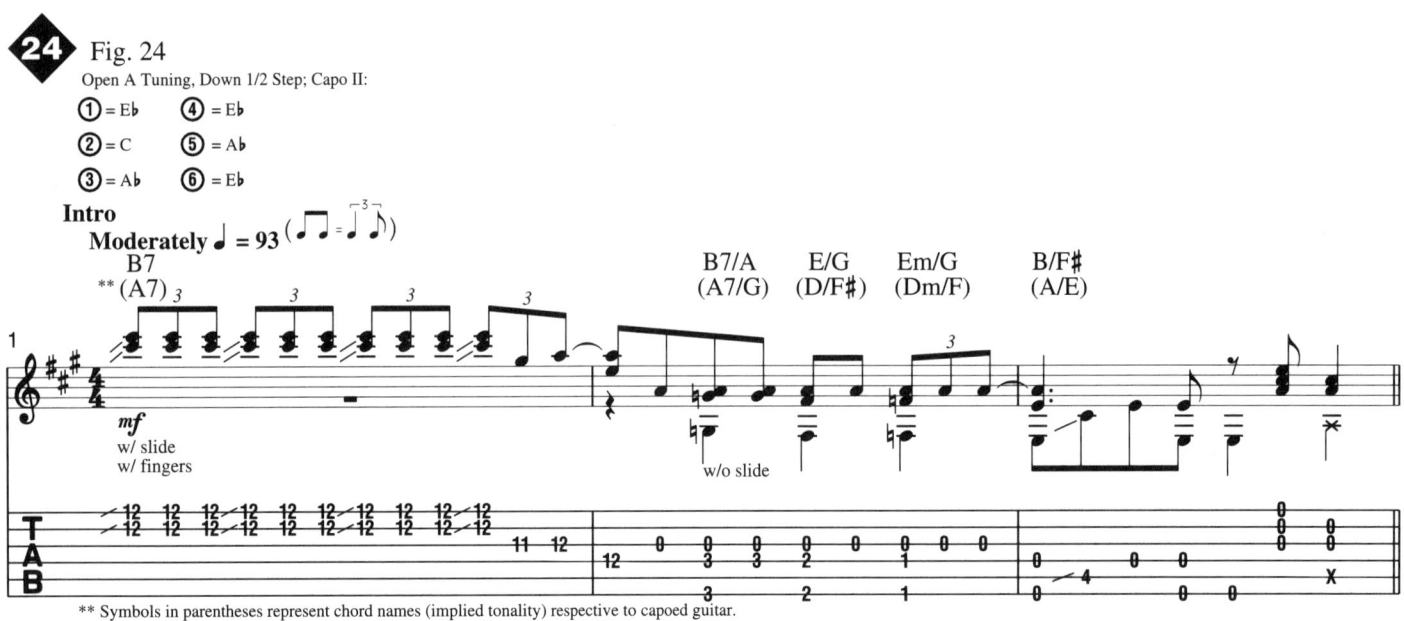

** Symbols in parentheses represent chord names (implied tonality) respective to capoed guitar.
Symbols above reflect actual sounding chord. Capoed fret is "0" in TAB.

Copyright © (1978), 1990, 1991 King Of Spades Music
All Rights Reserved   Used by Permission

Fig. 25—Verse 3

Verse 3 contains the most standard 12-bar arrangement: I chord (4 measures), IV chord (2 measures), I chord (2 measures), V chord (1 measure), IV chord (1 measure), and I chord (2 measures). The form is similar to verse 1 except for measures 5 and 6 (IV chord) where Johnson barres a 2nd inversion triad with his index finger while pulling-off and hammering notes from the D Mixolydian mode on string 1. Can you imagine how "modern" this must have sounded in the late thirties?

Fig. 26—Verse 4

Though all 5 verses are nearly identical (see Fig. 25 for one exception), the IV chord (measures 5 and 6) in verse 4 also has a unique spin. Johnson snaps string 5 (like a contemporary funk bass player!) on beats 1 and 3 in each measure while leaving musical space for the remaining beats.

PREACHIN' BLUES (UP JUMPED THE DEVIL)
SA 2632-1
Words and Music by Robert Johnson
(Recorded Friday, November 27, 1936 in San Antonio, Texas)

Fig. 27—Intro and Verse 1

In the history of popular American music there are certain virtuoso performances that represent a benchmark for the instrument and the genre. A short, selected list would include the following: the boogie woogie piano of Albert Ammons on "Boogie Woogie Stomp," the alto saxophone of Charlie Parker on "Cool Blues," the tenor saxophone of John Coltrane on "Giant Steps," the electric guitar of Jimi Hendrix on his version of the "Star Spangled Banner," and the acoustic slide guitar of Robert Johnson on "Preachin' Blues." This muscular tour-de-force is virtually without precedent in the blues before Johnson (or after, for that matter). Though obviously inspired by Son House's composition "Preachin' The Blues," it blows away all comparisons due to the driving energy, improvisational creativity, and unexcelled technique.

The 8-measure intro is divided into two sections. Measures 1-3 contain Johnson's typical slide intro with a measure of the octave and two measures of a descending turnaround pattern in open E, and "swing" more than the rest of the tune. Measure 4, with its open strings, functions as resolution to the I and as a transition measure to the second section of the intro. Note that it is also the template for the last measure in each verse, where it also functions as definite resolution and as a buffer between the intense riffing that occurs almost unabated throughout. Measures 5-8 introduce the vamp that is the basis for the entire tune.

Verse 1 is 18 measures long and, like the other four, consists of slide licks on the top strings (mainly around the octave) syncopated wildly with plucked open strings that maintain the I chord tonality.

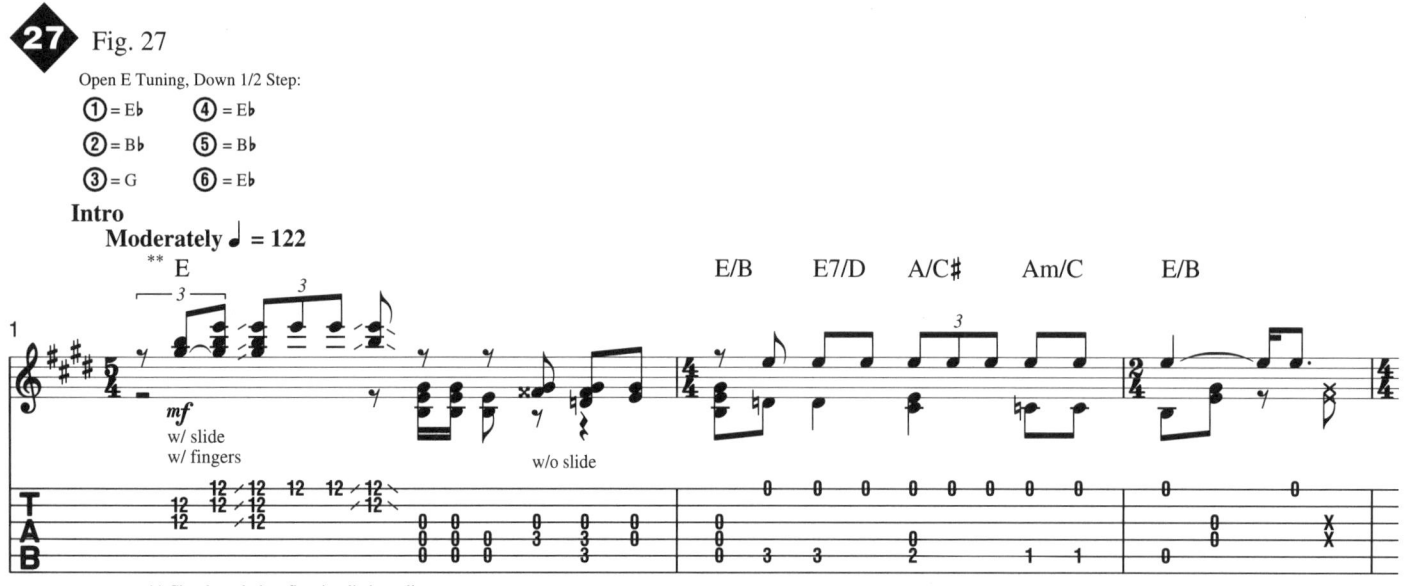

Copyright © (1978), 1990, 1991 King Of Spades Music
All Rights Reserved   Used by Permission

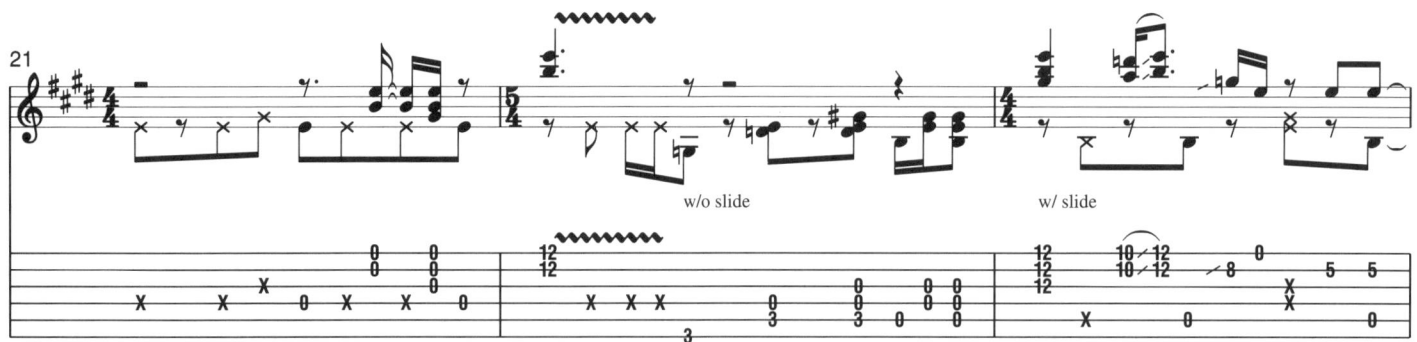

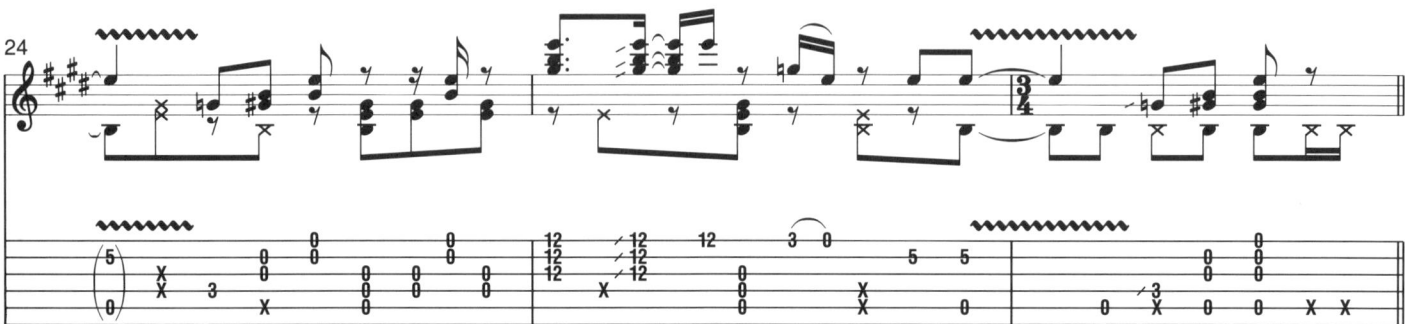

Fig. 28—Verse 2

All five verses are similar; however, they are not identical. Verse 2, with 17 measures, shows just some of the subtle variations that Johnson throws in as the song progresses. For instance, dig the sixteenth-note strum of measure 1. Likewise, notice the turnaround-type pattern in measure 13 and the little pull-off lick in measure 14. Both examples are fretted with the fingers.

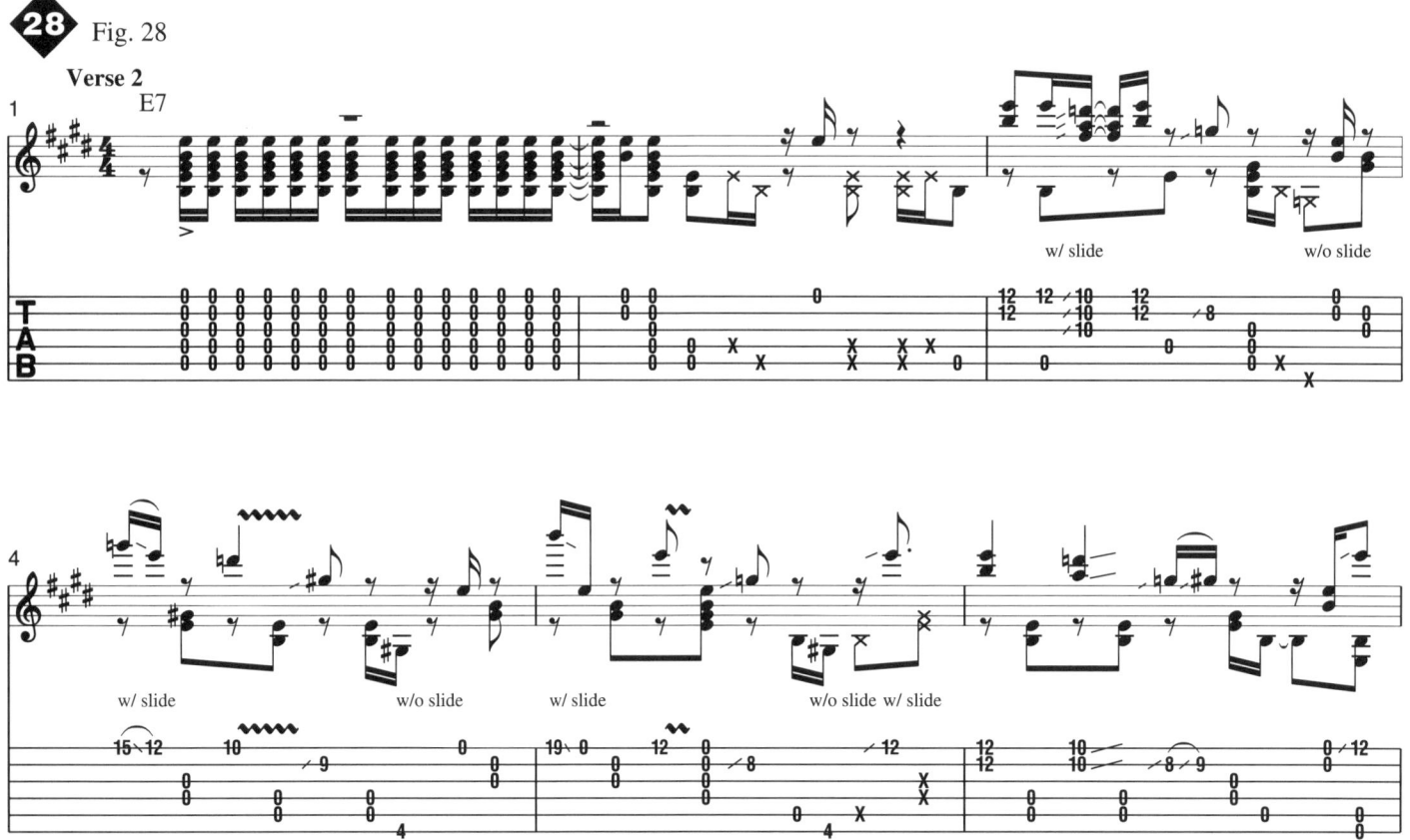

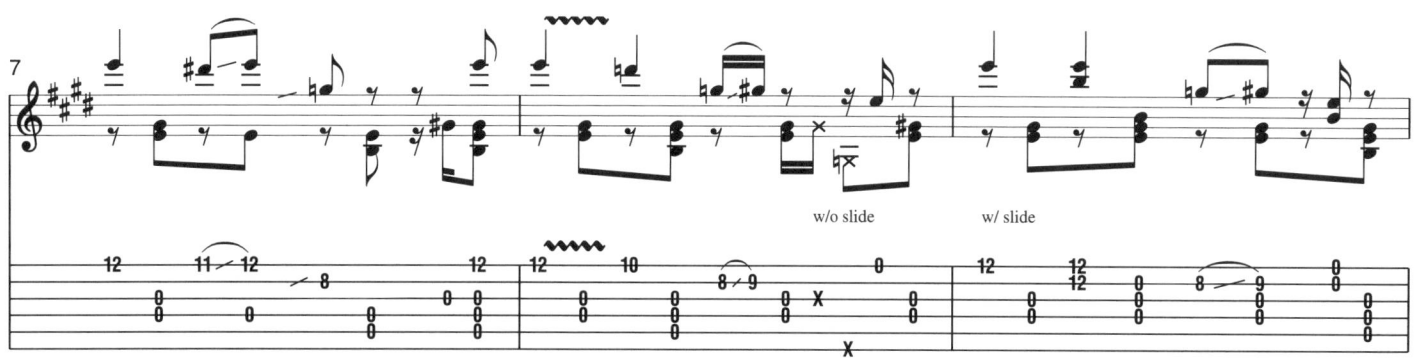

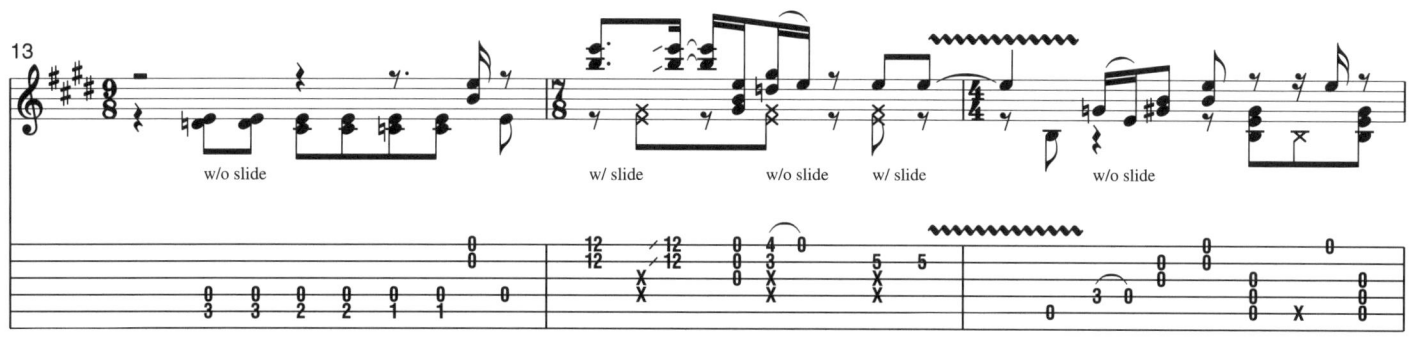
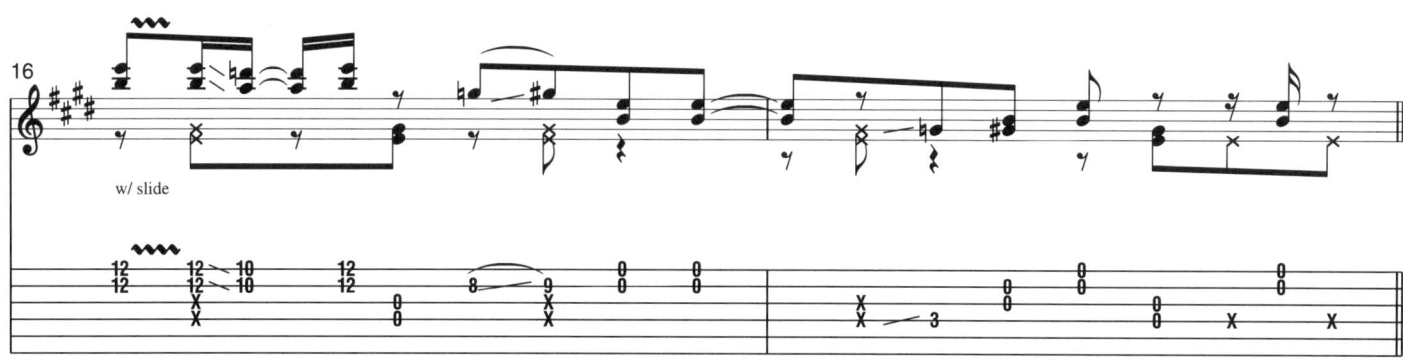

47

IF I HAD POSSESSION OVER JUDGMENT DAY
SA 2633-1
Words and Music by Robert Johnson
(Recorded Friday, November 27, 1936 in San Antonio, Texas)

Fig. 29—Intro and Verse 1

"If I Had Possession Over Judgment Day," Johnson's take on "Rollin' and Tumblin'," has a jaunty, lilting rhythmic bent that is in direct contrast to the measured meter of Hambone Willie Newbern's "Roll and Tumble Blues" from 1929. It was the last song Johnson recorded at his last session in 1936. Perhaps not knowing whether he would get another chance to show what he could do, Johnson strutted his stuff for all the world to hear. Ironically, this number would not be released until 1961 when Columbia gathered a selection of his compositions on LP.

Like the majority of his open-tuned slide pieces, Johnson liberally mixed fretted notes with application of the bottleneck. The 3-measure intro starts with his typical octave lick on the top two strings followed by a descending turnaround pattern with bass-string octaves. In measure 3, he resolves to the tonic notes. The 17-measure verse could be seen as a more conventional 16-measure form if you combine the two measures in 2/4 time into one measure of 4/4. As written, though, the arrangement for verses 1 and 3 is as follows: I chord = 6 measures, IV chord = 2 measures, I chord = 3 measures, V chord = 1 measure, IV chord = 1 measure, I chord = 4 measures. Verses 2, 4, and 5 begin with 11 measures of the I chord.

The "response" part of the "call (vocal) and response" section (I chord) is a challenging combination of syncopated slide licks and syncopated, fretted bass notes. Johnson nails the V and IV chords by playing the chord tones at frets 7 and 5, respectively.

In verse 1, he begins with a slide lick at fret 5 that *could* imply the 3rd and 5th of the IV (D) chord, but verses 2, 4, and 5 all begin with the octave slide lick indicating the tonic chord. In verse 3, Johnson substitutes the open strings (in essence, the tonic chord an octave lower) for the octave slide lick.

Fig. 30—Verse 5

Verse 5 (the last verse) is 16 measures long due to the final I-chord change spanning 3 measures. Check out measure 6 where Johnson flies up past the end of the fingerboard, over the *soundhole,* and whips his slide down through (what would be) frets 25, 24, 23, 22, and 20 before resolving to the octave in measure 8. Smokin'!

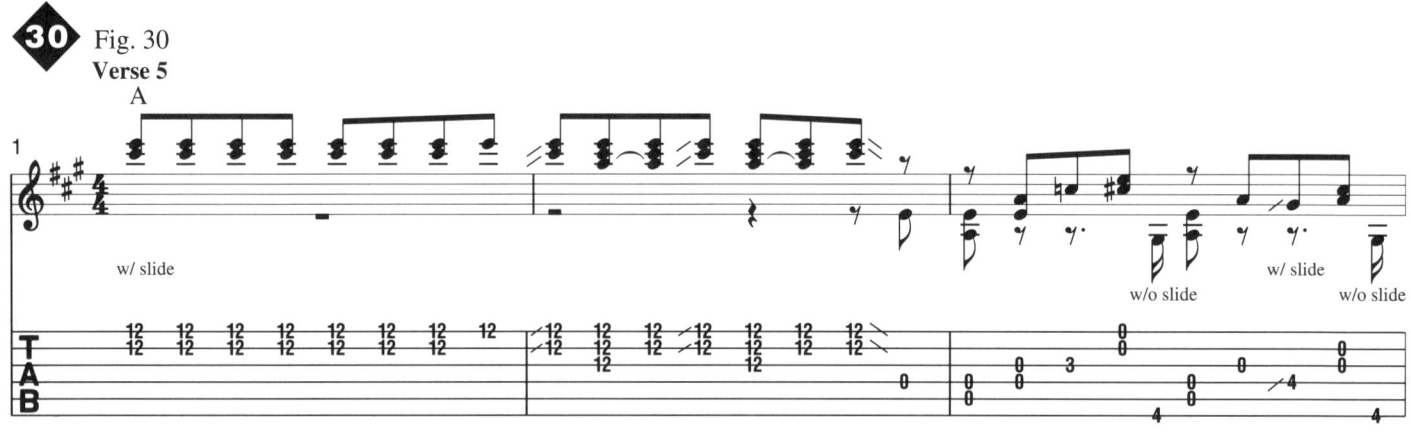

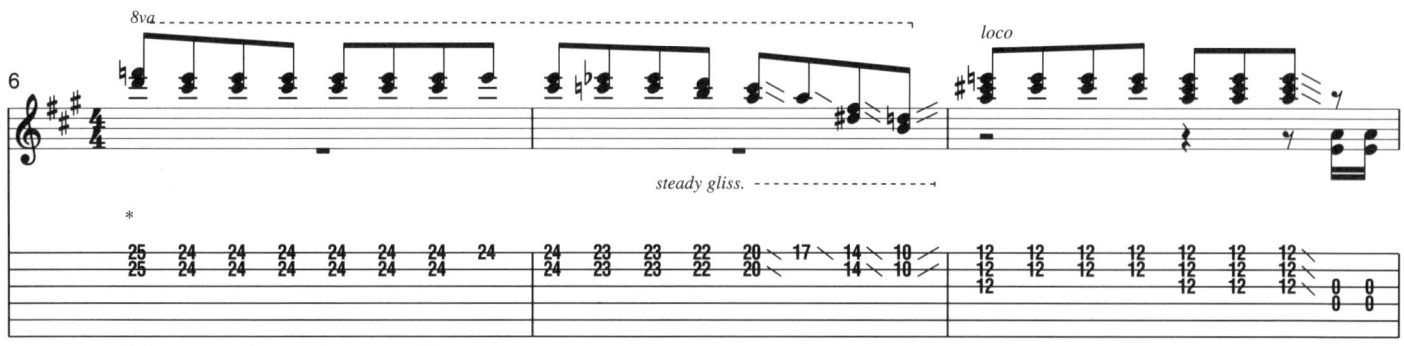

** Position slide where imaginary fret would be.

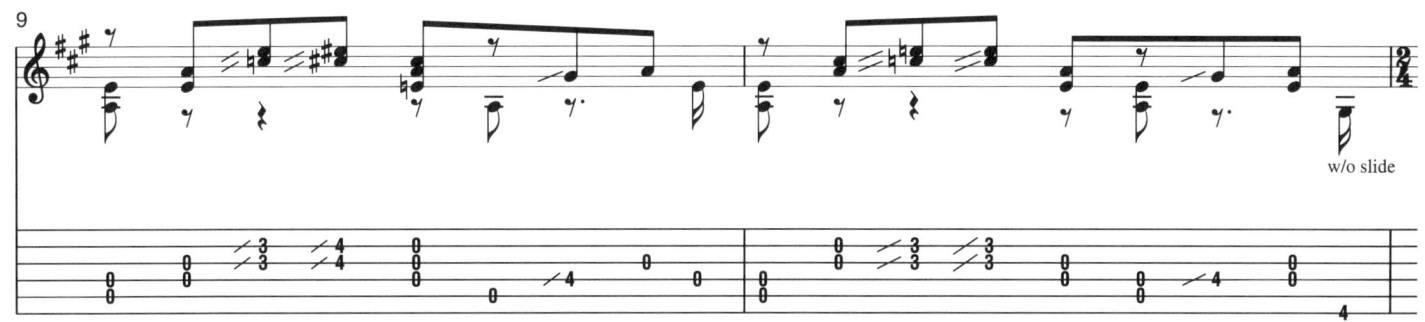
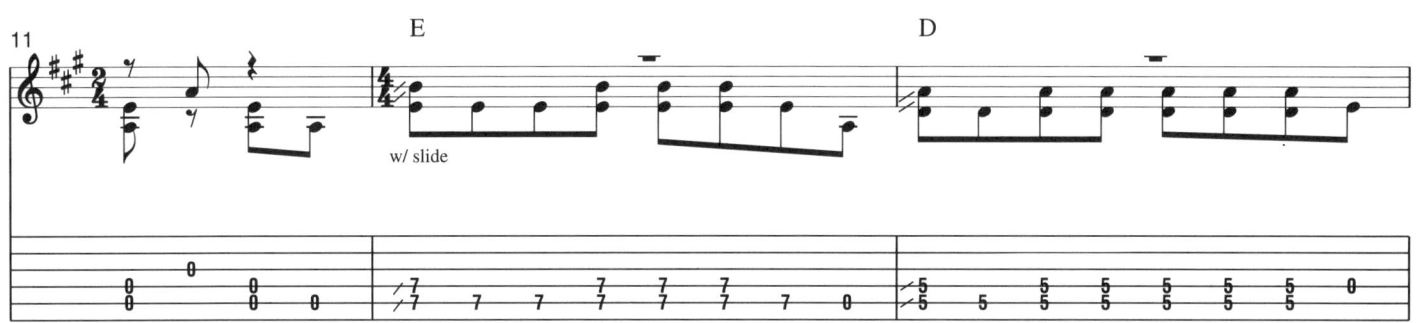
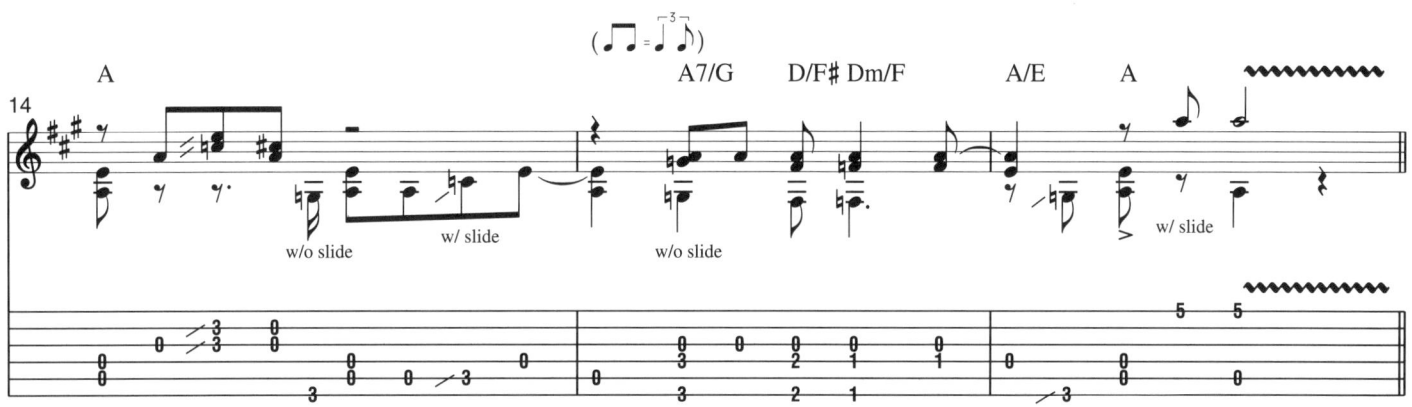

I'M A STEADY ROLLIN' MAN (STEADY ROLLIN' MAN)

DAL 378-1

Words and Music by Robert Johnson
(Recorded Saturday, June 19, 1937 in Dallas, Texas)

Fig. 31—Intro and Verse 1

"Steady Rollin' Man" was one of four tunes recorded at Robert Johnson's first Dallas session. Over six months had passed since his last San Antonio date and his playing overall shows confidence. It is likely Johnson was recording with the Gibson L-1 pictured in the studio photograph, as none of the songs recorded in Dallas use a capo.

Though it employs precious few bass string boogie patterns, "Steady Rollin' Man" has a perfectly relaxed shuffle rhythm that Johnson had been perfecting over the years. It takes little effort to imagine this piece arranged for an electric blues combo ten years hence in Chicago!

The 4-measure intro contains the "Robert Johnson double turnaround" with descending triple-stop dominant chords in measures 1 and 2 and the descending bass string/pedal tone pattern in measures 3 and 4. The verse consists of string 5 open (A) with either the 5th (E) or 6th (F♯) on string 4. The root (A), ♭7th (G), and 3rd (C♯) are played on top as a hook for the I chord. For the IV chord Johnson makes only a subtle change for the bass accompaniment where he uses string 5 open with the F♯ (3rd of D) on string 4. To the top-string melody he now adds in the root (D) in place of the C♯. The V chord is indicated quite minimally with the 5th (B) and root (E) notes on the bass strings and the same notes up an octave on strings 1 and 2. Instead of resolving to the V chord, measures 11 and 12 of the turnaround repeat a phrase similar to measures 3 and 4 of the I chord. Verses 2, 3, and 4 are similar to verse 1.

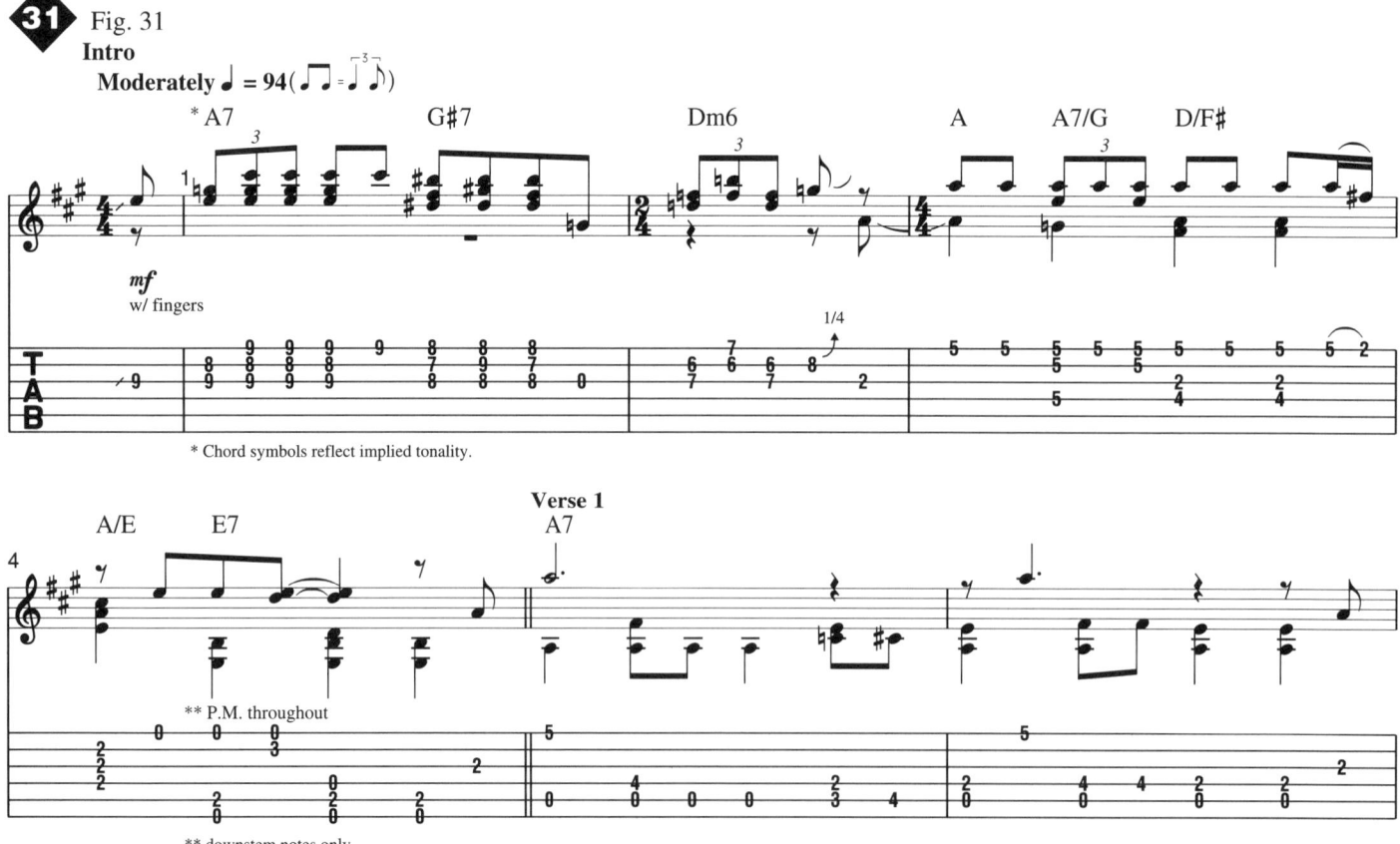

Copyright © (1978), 1990, 1991 King Of Spades Music
All Rights Reserved   Used by Permission

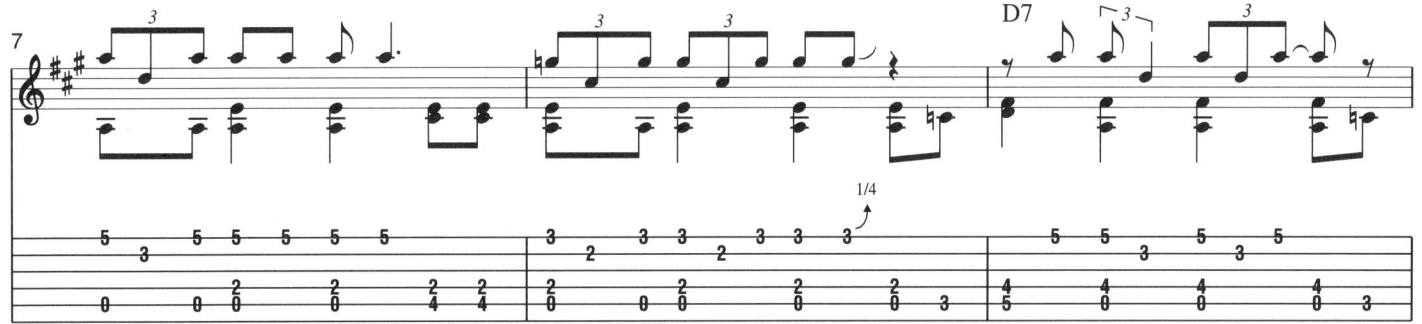

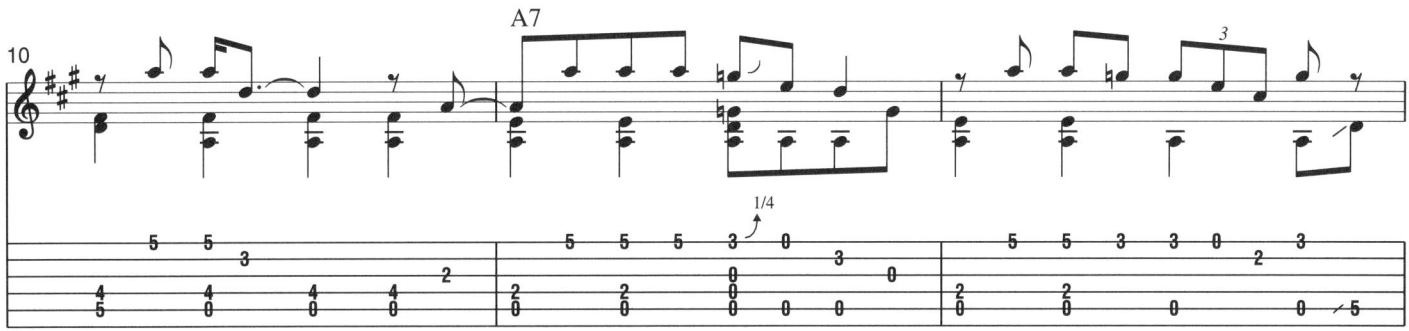

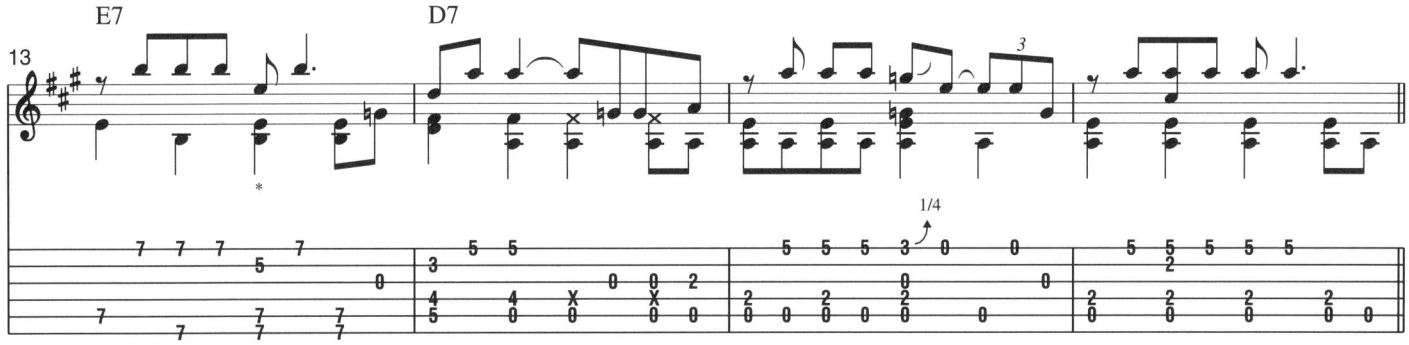

* downstem double stop played with 3rd finger of left hand

Fig. 32—Verse 5

Verse 5 is basically the same as verses 2-4 up to measures 13 and 14 where Johnson tags on two measures similar to measures 3 and 4 of the intro. On beat 3 of measure 14 he ends his production with an open position A major chord.

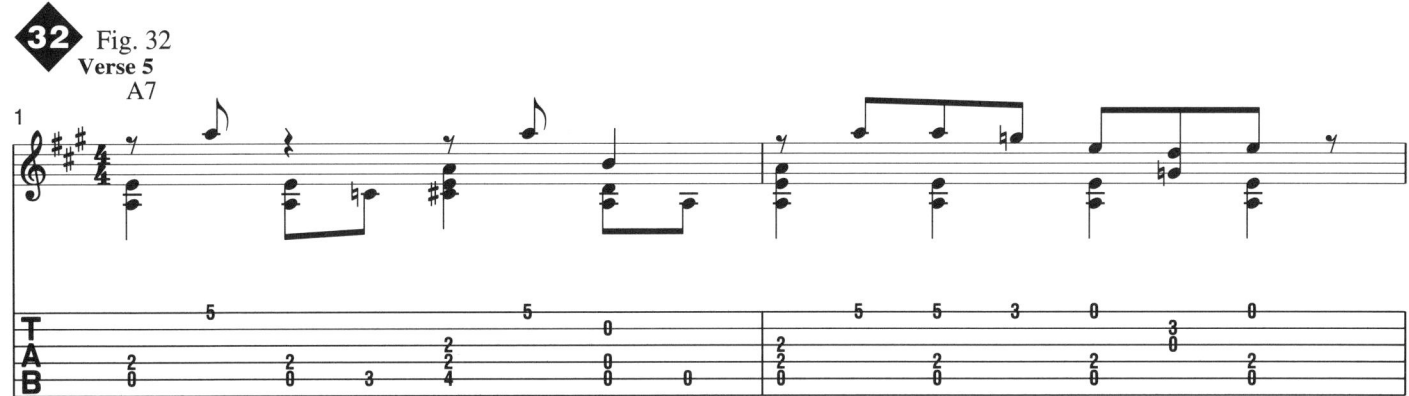

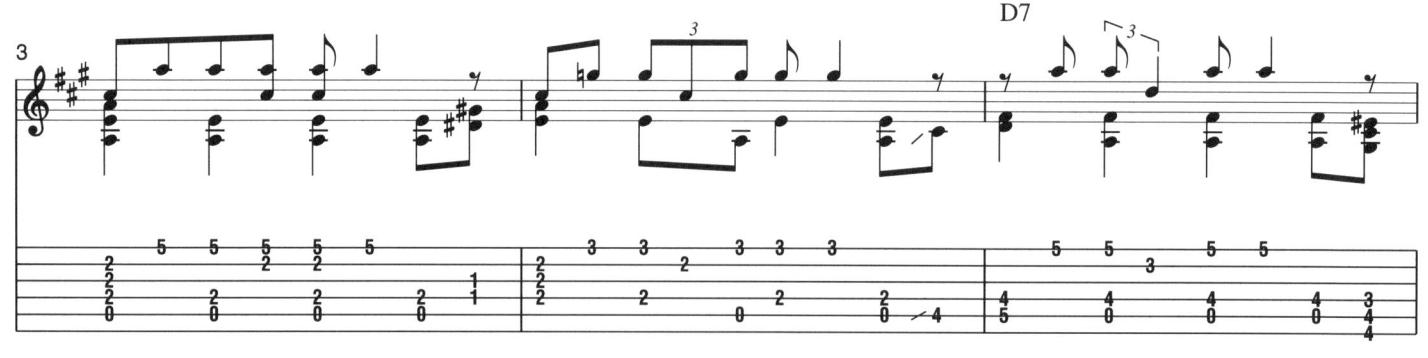
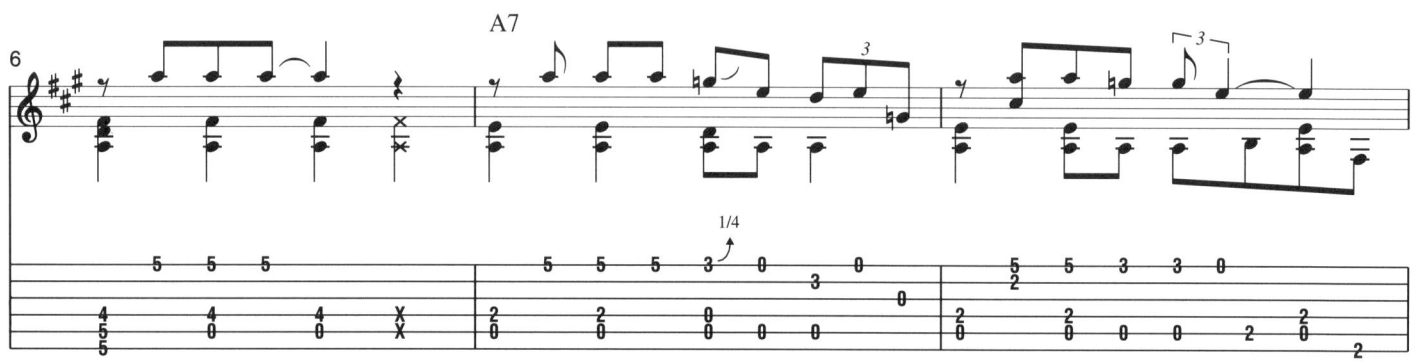
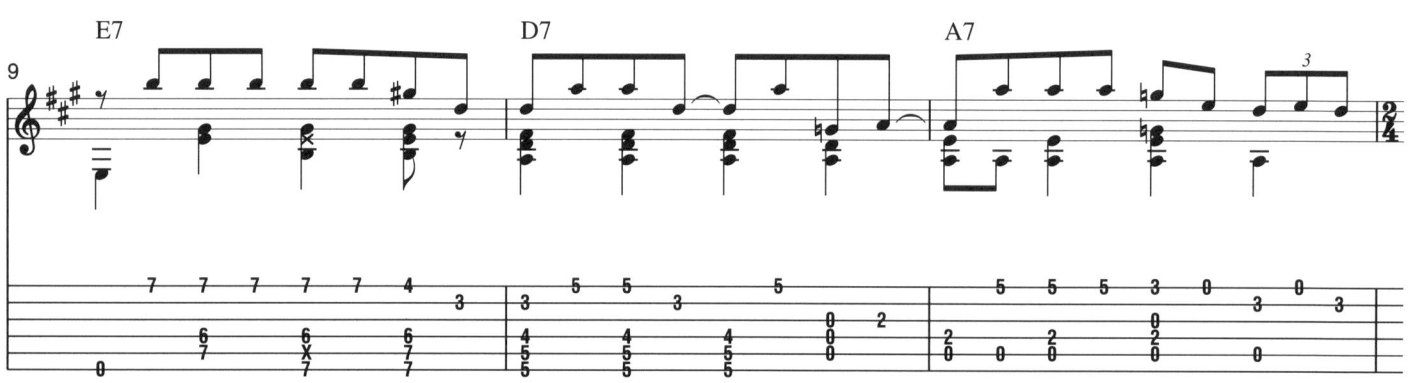
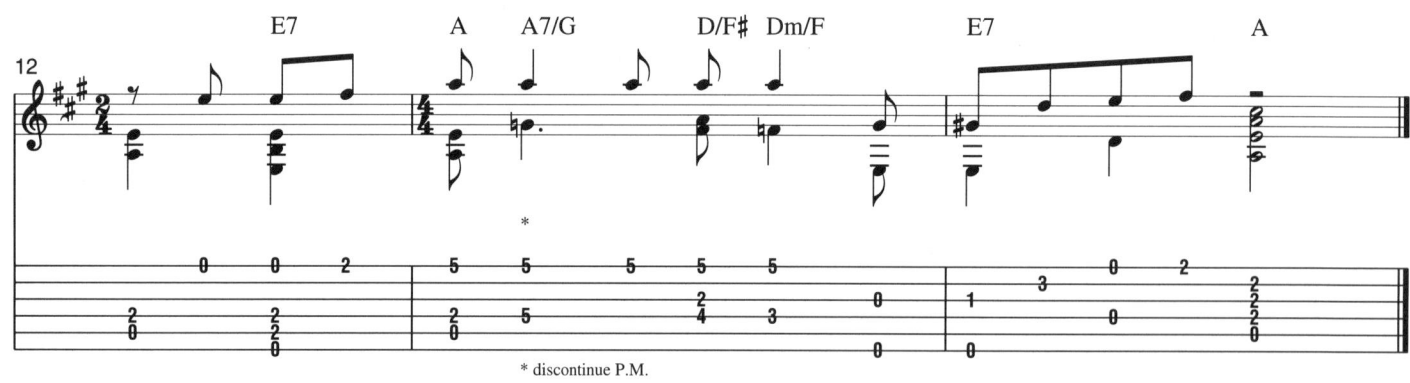

* discontinue P.M.

HELL HOUND ON MY TRAIL
DAL 394-2
Words and music by Robert Johnson
(Recorded Sunday, June 20, 1937 in Dallas, Texas)

Fig. 33—Intro and Verse 1

Along with "Cross Road Blues," "Hell Hound On My Trail" is the song that has influenced the Robert Johnson legend the most. It is a truly haunting composition and performance beyond the lyrical content, due in part to the floating nature of the verses without firm resolution to either the I or V chord. Another reason for the effect is the open Em tuning that he borrowed from Skip James and only uses this one time. Its employment is subtle but undeniable as Johnson interchanges the major 3rd with the ♭3rd. Most significantly, the sympathetic vibration of the open G string provides a melancholy, minor key presence even when it is not being struck or fretted.

The 4-measure intro uses the same triple-stop dominant forms in measures 1 and 2 that Johnson regularly plays in his standard-tuned numbers. He can do this because the top three strings in open Em tuning correspond to the top three strings in standard tuning. Measures 3 and 4, however, employ the descending/pedal tone turnaround pattern that ends on the I chord. This 2-measure phrase and its 1-measure variation function as a repeating theme throughout the verses.

The verse structure of "Hell Hound On My Trail" is based on I-V chord changes with the descending pattern interjected three times as musical release from the tension engendered by the repeating I chord (E7) phrases. There is no change to the IV chord. Verses 1 and 2, though they contain 17 and 15 measures respectively, follow the same arrangement: I, V, I, turnaround, I, turnaround, I, V, turnaround, I. Where they differ is in the number of repeats of the I chord and the turnaround pattern.

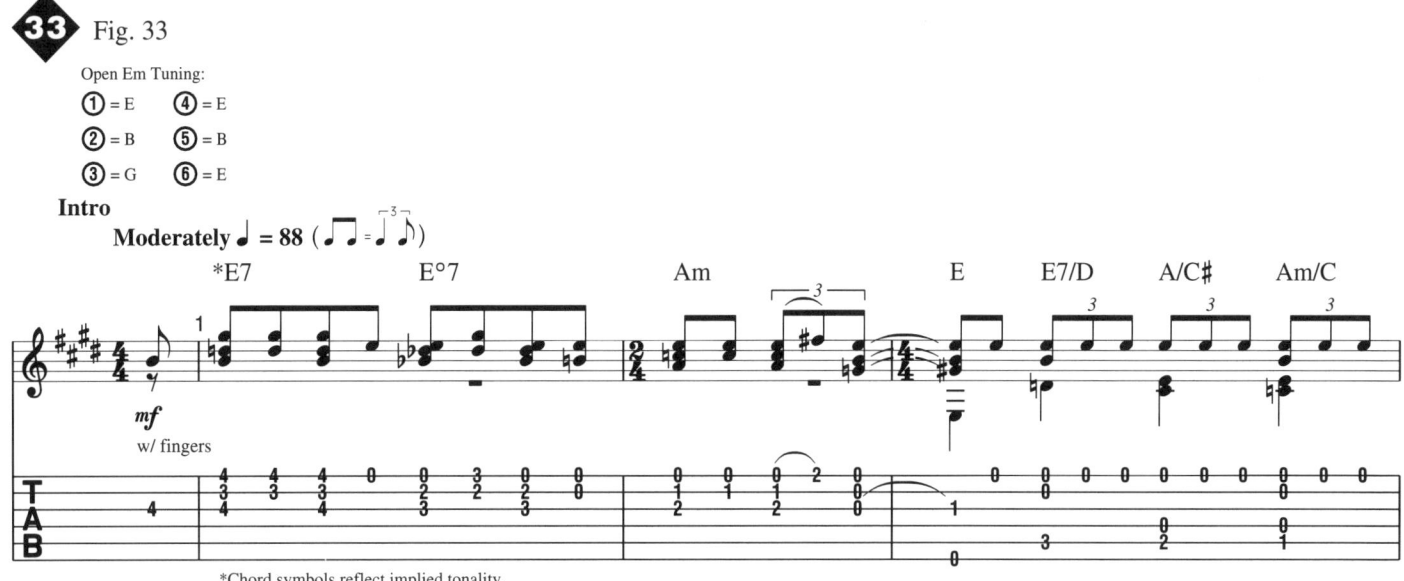

*Chord symbols reflect implied tonality.

Copyright © (1978), 1990, 1991 King Of Spades Music
All Rights Reserved   Used by Permission

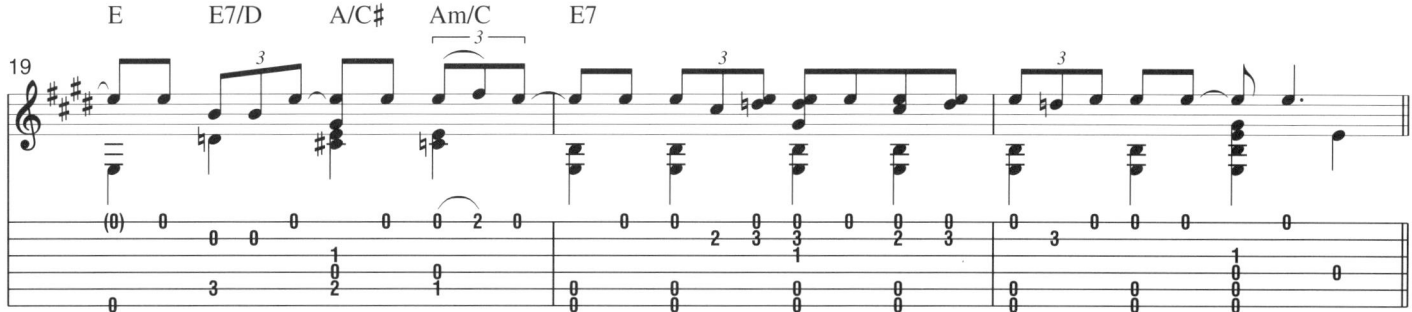

Fig. 34—Verse 3

Verse 3 contains 15 measures and follows a different arrangement: I, turnaround, I, turnaround, I, V, turnaround, I. Verse 4 is 17 measures in length but basically follows the same arrangement structure.

34 Fig. 34

Verse 3

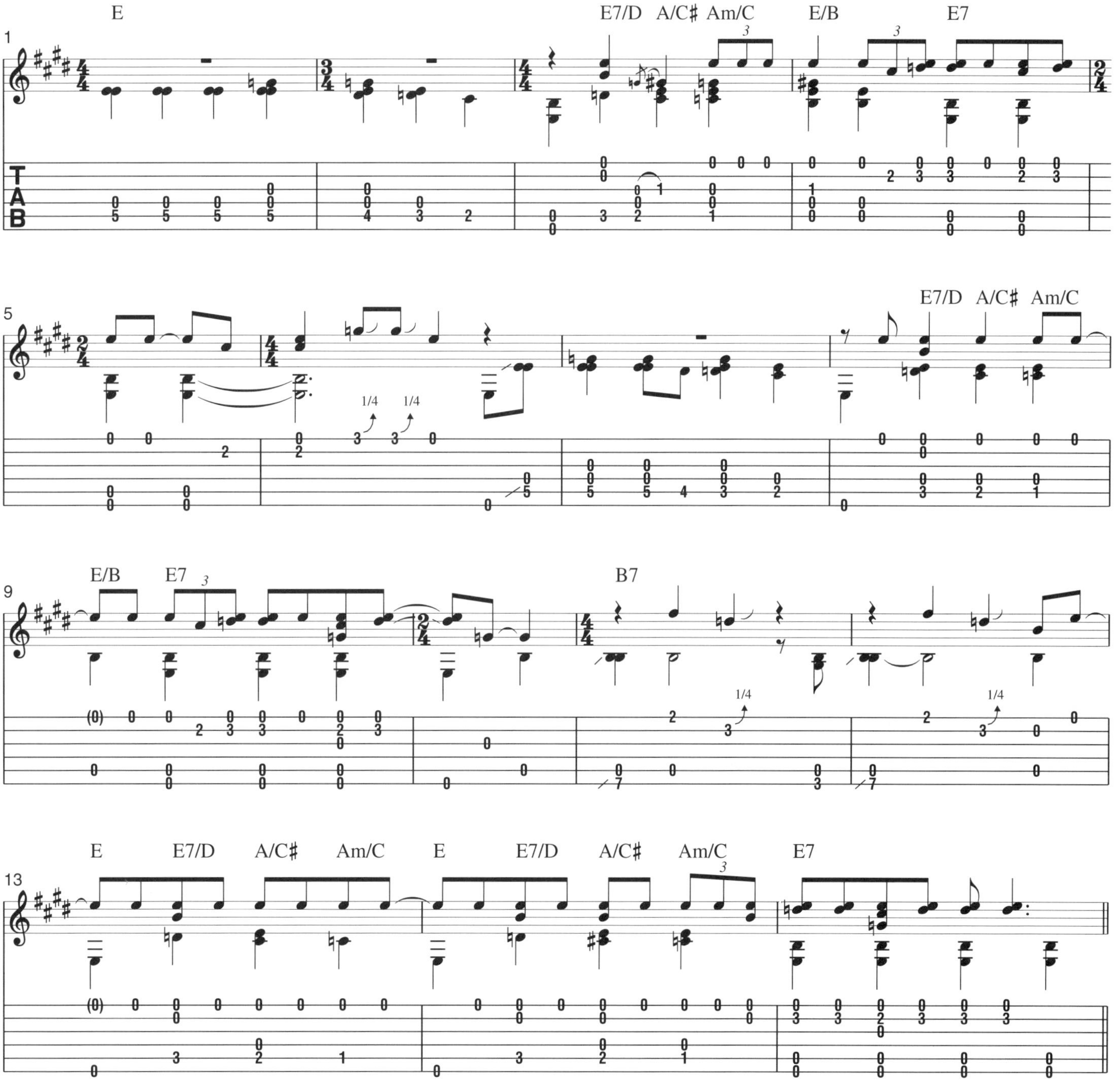

STOP BREAKIN' DOWN BLUES
DAL 399-1

Words and Music by Robert Johnson
(Recorded Sunday, June 20, 1937 in Dallas, Texas)

Fig. 35—Intro and Verse 1

"Stop Breakin' Down Blues" is unusual inasmuch as it is the only non-slide song in open A tuning. Except as noted, it also confirms the evolution in Johnson's music towards standard 12-bar arrangements. Somewhat similar in feel to "I'm A Steady Rollin' Man," it swings and shuffles sans the use of cut boogie patterns.

The 2-measure intro contains a "fast" version of the descending turnaround pattern (1 measure long) that resolves to the tonic (I) chord, and a measure similar to the increment for the I chord. The 12-bar form of verse 1 repeats the A major increment for the I chord change except in measure 8, where the ♭7th (G) is introduced to indicate movement from A to A7. The IV chord employs a D7 barre chord phrase at fret 5, also in 1-measure increments. The V chord is similar to the IV chord, but 2 frets higher on the fingerboard. Measures 11 and 12, where the turnaround would normally appear, contain 2 measures of the I-chord lick.

Copyright © (1978), 1990, 1991 King Of Spades Music
All Rights Reserved   Used by Permission

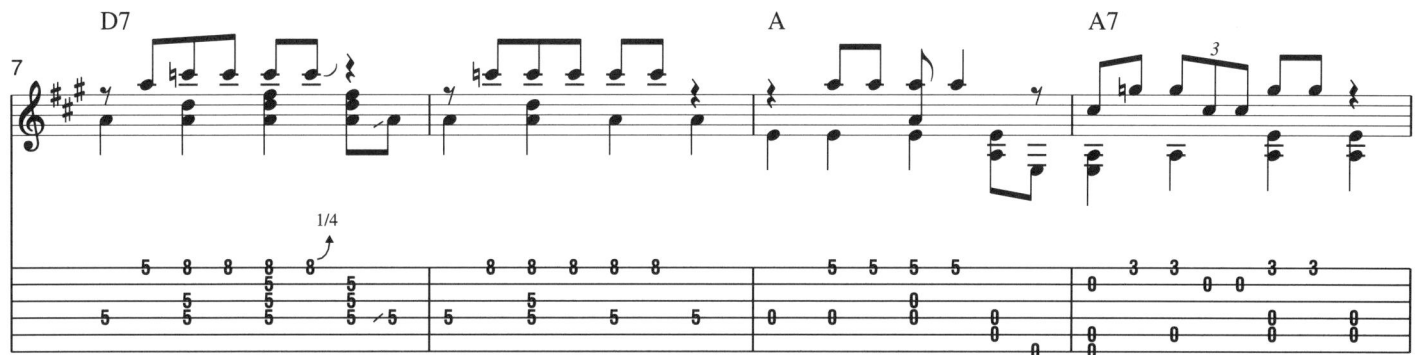

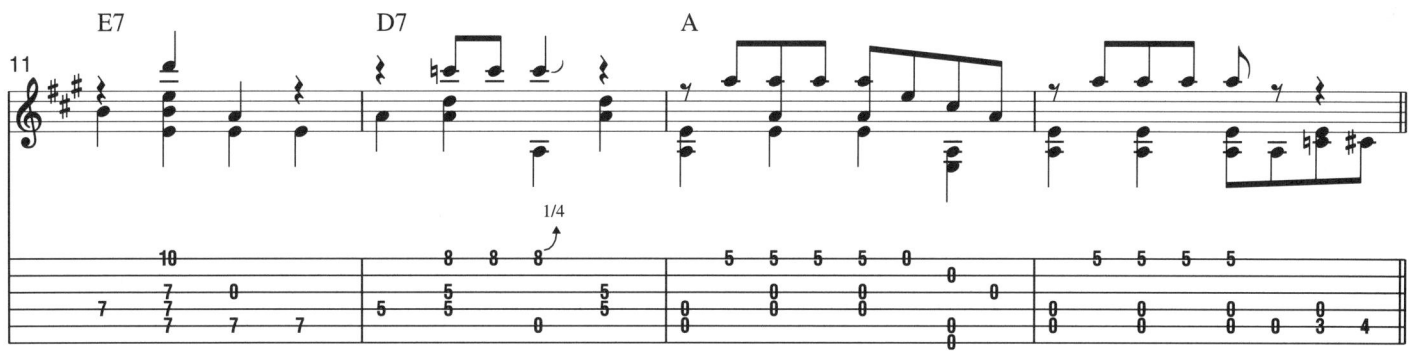

Fig. 36—Verse 3

Verse 3 is virtually identical to verse 1 except for a 2-measure tag following the regular 12-bar blues form. Although similar to the I-chord increments used throughout, measure 13 includes the ♭9th (B♭) that *may* be a mistake. Conversely, measure 14 has the major 7th (G♯) which sounds more deliberate and is extremely hip for a Delta blues!

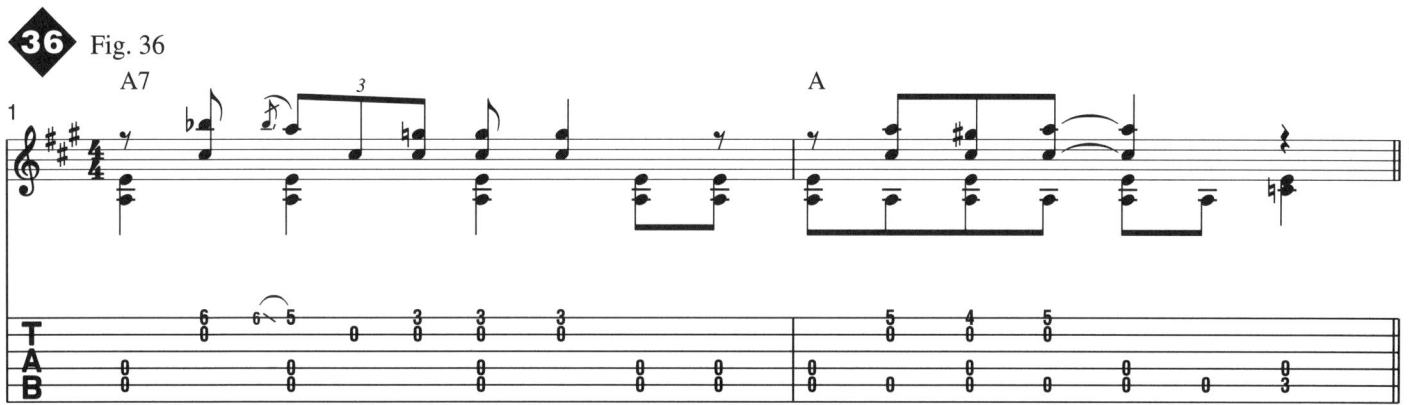

LOVE IN VAIN BLUES
DAL 402-1
Words and Music by Robert Johnson
(Recorded Sunday, June 20, 1937 in Dallas, Texas)

Fig. 37—Intro and Verse 1

Due to the prominent cover of "Love In Vain Blues" by the Rolling Stones in 1969 it has received an extra measure of attention. On its own merits, however, it occupies a unique spot in the Robert Johnson canon. First off, it is the only song he recorded in open G tuning, which is doubly unusual because it was such a common tuning for acoustic country blues. In addition, though a 12-bar blues, it is his only progression that incorporates II-V chord changes. Lastly, the recording from the CD box set contains the only known snippet of Johnson speaking as he introduces the song with, "I wanna go on with our next one myself." What was he referring to? We will never know for sure, but perhaps it was simply a matter that he did not want to stop the session yet and was ready to keep rolling.

The 4-measure intro is, structurally, the classic Robert Johnson double turn-around. Measures 1 and 2, though, contain a descending double-stop pattern on strings 1 and 2 that does not appear anywhere else in his music. It is interesting to note that at this point in his development he had found a way to reduce his chordal turnarounds to the bare minimum. Measures 3 and 4 utilize the descending pedal-point pattern that resolves to a D7 chord and functions as the turnaround in measures 11 and 12 for verses 1-3.

All four verses contain the following arrangement: I = 4 measures, IV = 2 measures, I = 2 measures, II = 1 measure, V = 1 measure, I = 1 measure, V = I measure. All of the changes are built around the appropriate chord form with very little left-hand embellishment. Note that Johnson throws in the V chord as a substitute for beats 3 and 4 of measure 5 (I chord).

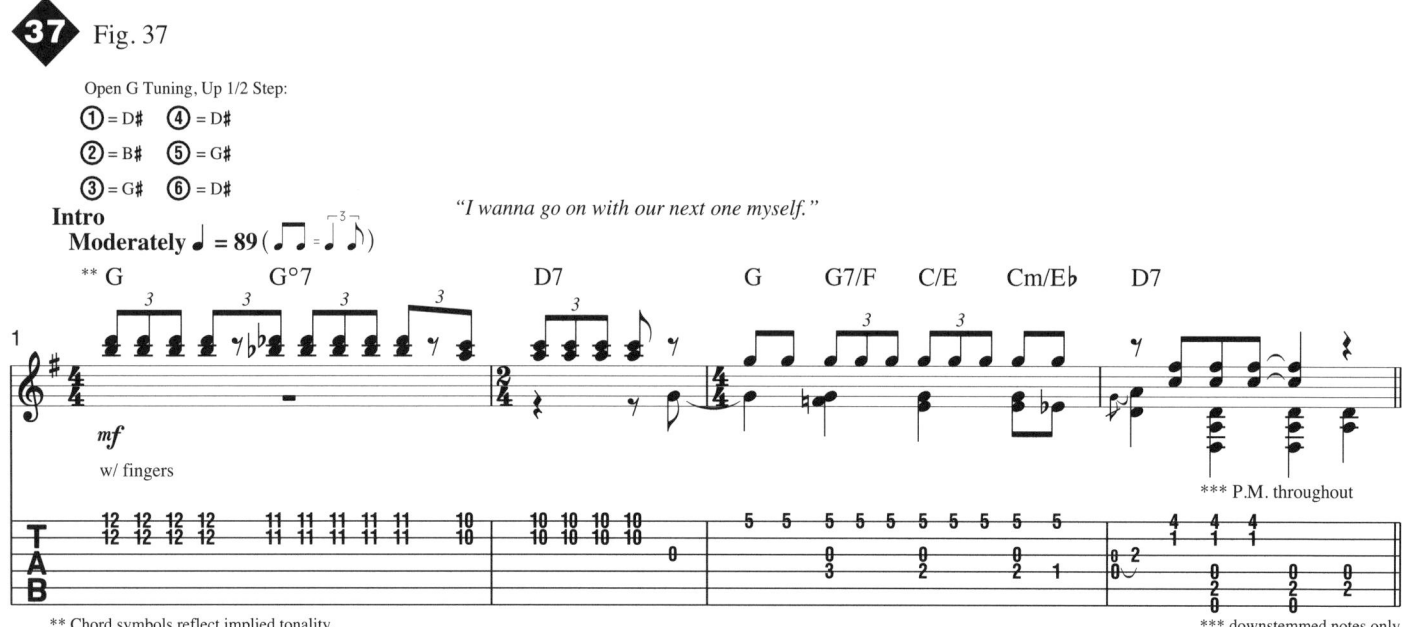

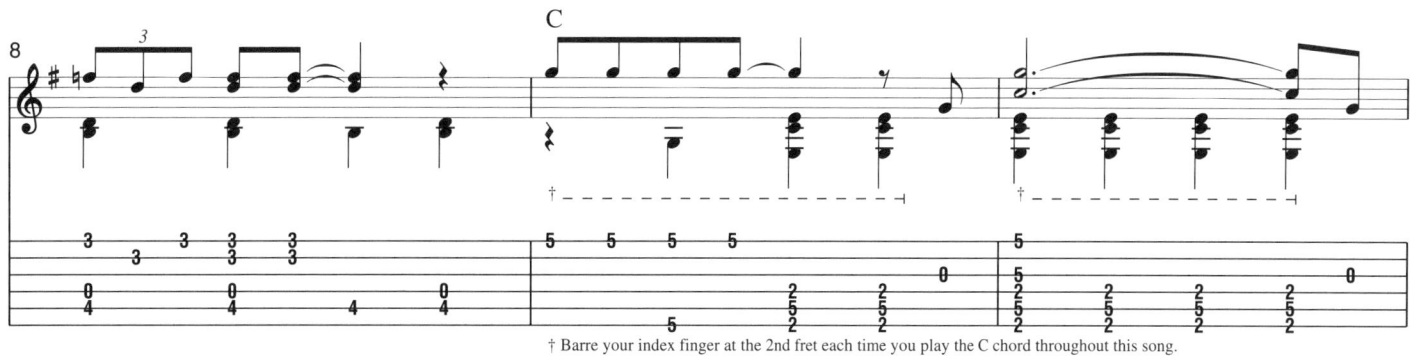

† Barre your index finger at the 2nd fret each time you play the C chord throughout this song.

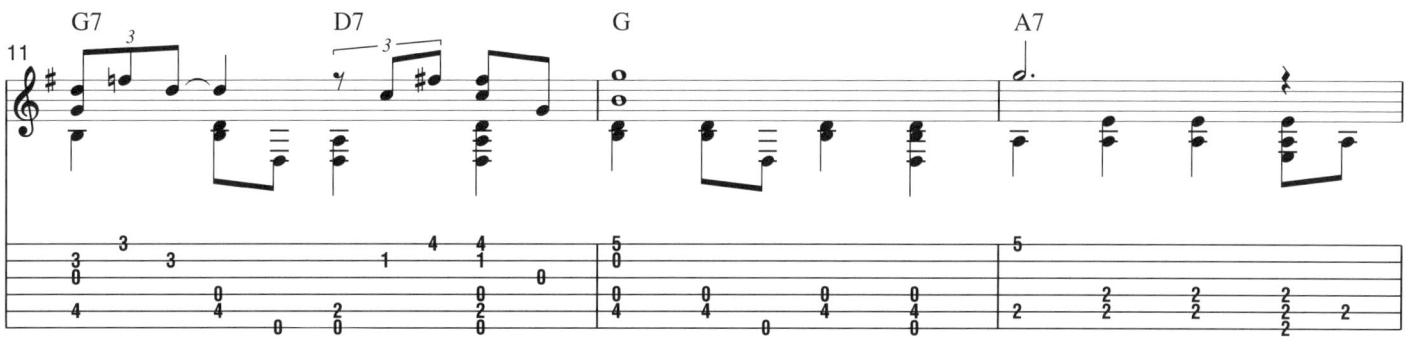
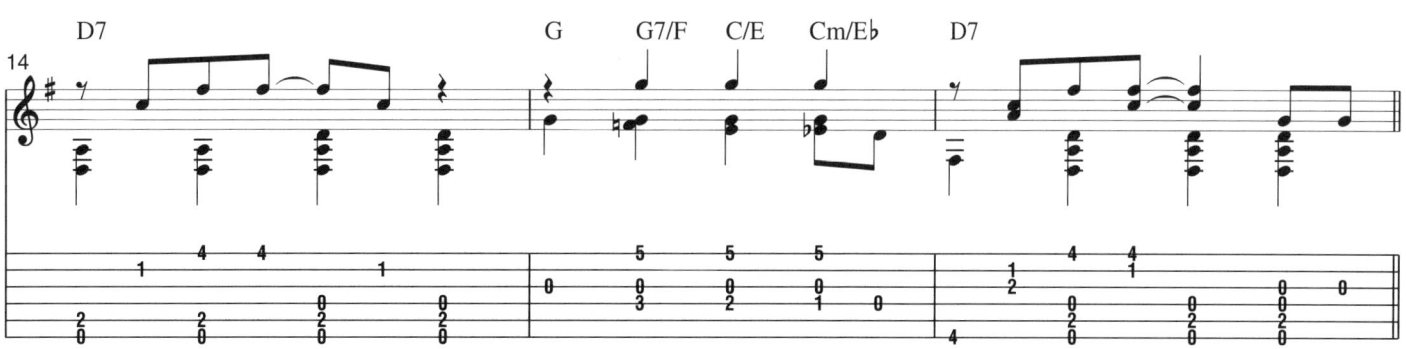

Guitar Notation Legend

Guitar Music can be notated three different ways: on a *musical staff*, in *tablature*, and in *rhythm slashes*.

RHYTHM SLASHES are written above the staff. Strum chords in the rhythm indicated. Use the chord diagrams found at the top of the first page of the transcription for the appropriate chord voicings. Round noteheads indicate single notes.

THE MUSICAL STAFF shows pitches and rhythms and is divided by bar lines into measures. Pitches are named after the first seven letters of the alphabet.

TABLATURE graphically represents the guitar fingerboard. Each horizontal line represents a a string, and each number represents a fret.

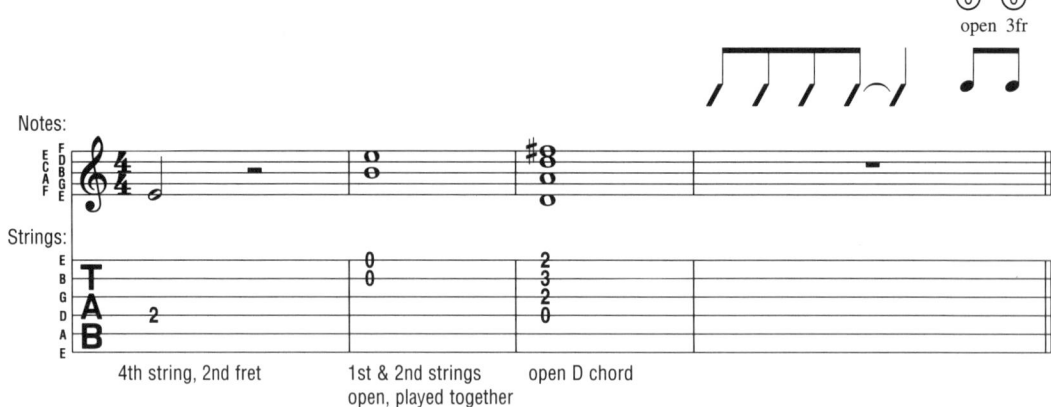

Definitions for Special Guitar Notation

HALF-STEP BEND: Strike the note and bend up 1/2 step.

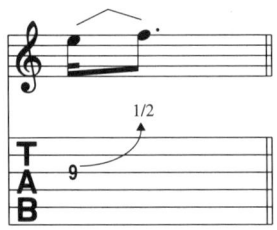

WHOLE-STEP BEND: Strike the note and bend up one step.

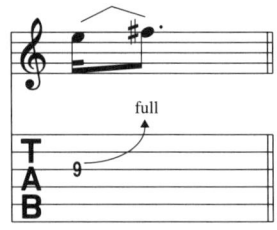

GRACE NOTE BEND: Strike the note and bend up as indicated. The first note does not take up any time.

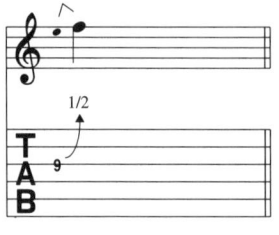

SLIGHT (MICROTONE) BEND: Strike the note and bend up 1/4 step.

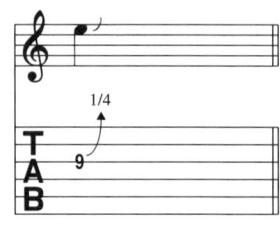

BEND AND RELEASE: Strike the note and bend up as indicated, then release back to the original note. Only the first note is struck.

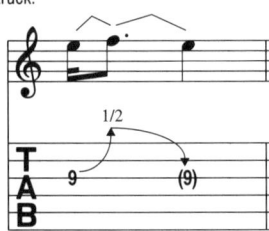

PRE-BEND: Bend the note as indicated, then strike it.

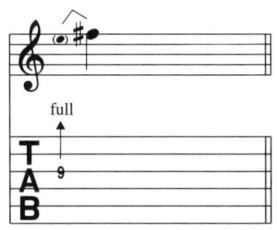

PRE-BEND AND RELEASE: Bend the note as indicated. Strike it and release the bend back to the original note.

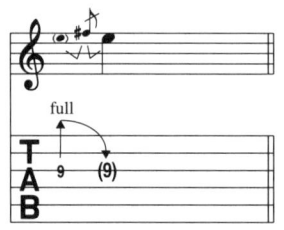

UNISON BEND: Strike the two notes simultaneously and bend the lower note up to the pitch of the higher.

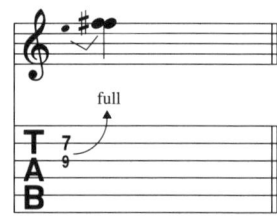

VIBRATO: The string is vibrated by rapidly bending and releasing the note with the fretting hand.

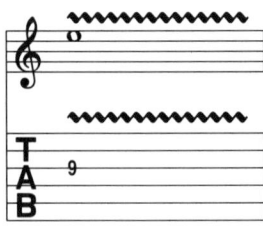

WIDE VIBRATO: The pitch is varied to a greater degree by vibrating with the fretting hand.

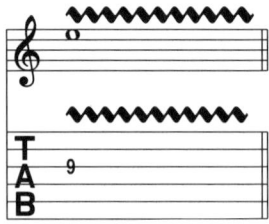

HAMMER-ON: Strike the first (lower) note with one finger, then sound the higher note (on the same string) with another finger by fretting it without picking.

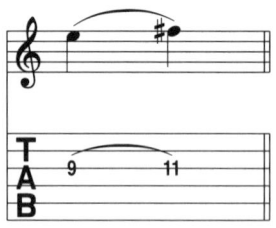

PULL-OFF: Place both fingers on the notes to be sounded. Strike the first note and without picking, pull the finger off to sound the second (lower) note.

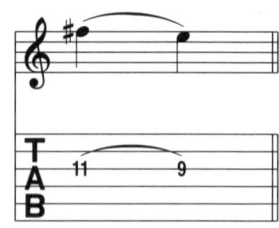

LEGATO SLIDE: Strike the first note and then slide the same fret-hand finger up or down to the second note. The second note is not struck.

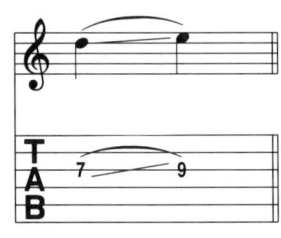

SHIFT SLIDE: Same as legato slide, except the second note is struck.

TRILL: Very rapidly alternate between the notes indicated by continuously hammering on and pulling off.

TAPPING: Hammer ("tap") the fret indicated with the pick-hand index or middle finger and pull off to the note fretted by the fret hand.

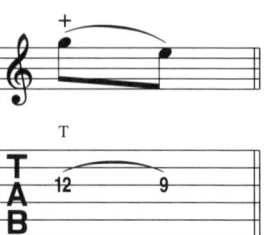

NATURAL HARMONIC: Strike the note while the fret-hand lightly touches the string directly over the fret indicated.

PINCH HARMONIC: The note is fretted normally and a harmonic is produced by adding the edge of the thumb or the tip of the index finger of the pick hand to the normal pick attack.

HARP HARMONIC: The note is fretted normally and a harmonic is produced by gently resting the pick hand's index finger directly above the indicated fret (in parentheses) while the pick hand's thumb or pick assists by plucking the appropriate string.

PICK SCRAPE: The edge of the pick is rubbed down (or up) the string, producing a scratchy sound.

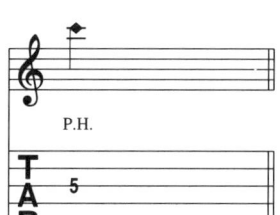
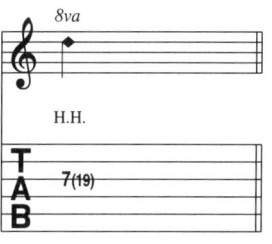

MUFFLED STRINGS: A percussive sound is produced by laying the fret hand across the string(s) without depressing, and striking them with the pick hand.

PALM MUTING: The note is partially muted by the pick hand lightly touching the string(s) just before the bridge.

RAKE: Drag the pick across the strings indicated with a single motion.

TREMOLO PICKING: The note is picked as rapidly and continuously as possible.

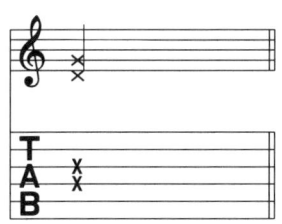
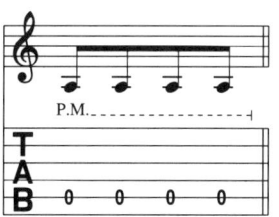
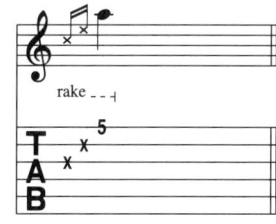

ARPEGGIATE: Play the notes of the chord indicated by quickly rolling them from bottom to top.

VIBRATO BAR DIVE AND RETURN: The pitch of the note or chord is dropped a specified number of steps (in rhythm) then returned to the original pitch.

VIBRATO BAR SCOOP: Depress the bar just before striking the note, then quickly release the bar.

VIBRATO BAR DIP: Strike the note and then immediately drop a specified number of steps, then release back to the original pitch.

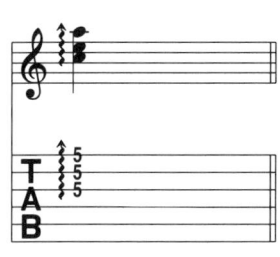
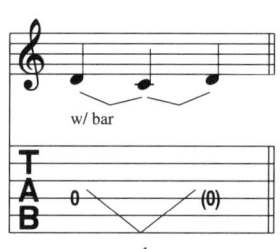

Additional Musical Definitions

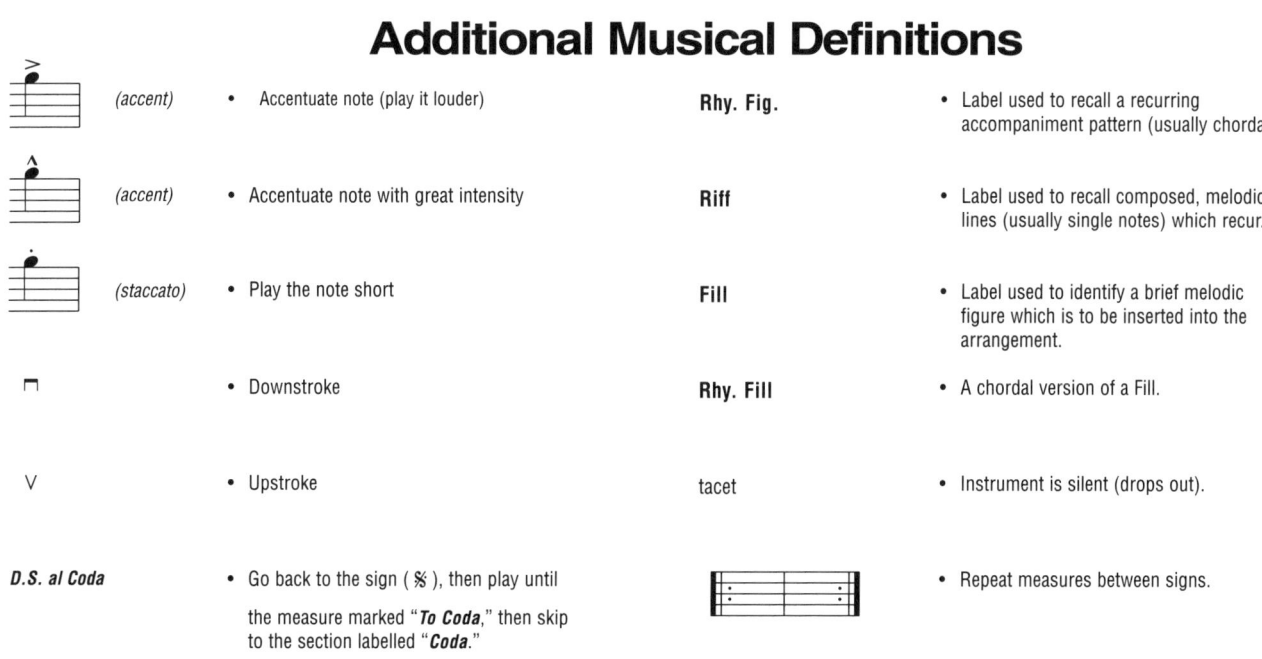

63

GUITAR *signature licks*

Signature Licks book/CD packs provide a step-by-step breakdown of "right from the record" riffs, licks, and solos so you can jam along with your favorite bands. They contain performance notes and an overview of each artist's or group's style, with note-for-note transcriptions in notes and tab. The CDs feature full-band demos at both normal and slow speeds.

BEST OF ACOUSTIC GUITAR
00695640 ....$19.95

AEROSMITH 1973-1979
00695106 ....$22.95

AEROSMITH 1979-1998
00695219 ....$22.95

BEST OF AGGRO-METAL
00695592 ....$19.95

BEST OF CHET ATKINS
00695752 ....$22.95

THE BEACH BOYS DEFINITIVE COLLECTION
00695683 ....$22.95

BEST OF THE BEATLES FOR ACOUSTIC GUITAR
00695453 ....$22.95

THE BEATLES BASS
00695283 ....$22.95

THE BEATLES FAVORITES
00695096 ....$24.95

THE BEATLES HITS
00695049 ....$24.95

BEST OF GEORGE BENSON
00695418 ....$22.95

BEST OF BLACK SABBATH
00695249 ....$22.95

BEST OF BLINK 182
00695704 ....$22.95

BEST OF BLUES GUITAR
00695846 ....$19.95

BLUES GUITAR CLASSICS
00695177 ....$19.95

BLUES/ROCK GUITAR MASTERS
00695348 ....$19.95

BEST OF CHARLIE CHRISTIAN
00695584 ....$22.95

BEST OF ERIC CLAPTON
00695038 ....$24.95

ERIC CLAPTON – THE BLUESMAN
00695040 ....$22.95

ERIC CLAPTON – FROM THE ALBUM UNPLUGGED
00695250 ....$24.95

BEST OF CREAM
00695251 ....$22.95

DEEP PURPLE – GREATEST HITS
00695625 ....$22.95

THE DOORS
00695373 ....$22.95

FAMOUS ROCK GUITAR SOLOS
00695590 ....$19.95

BEST OF FOO FIGHTERS
00695481 ....$22.95

GREATEST GUITAR SOLOS OF ALL TIME
00695301 ....$19.95

BEST OF GRANT GREEN
00695747 ....$22.95

GUITAR INSTRUMENTAL HITS
00695309 ....$19.95

GUITAR RIFFS OF THE '60S
00695218 ....$19.95

BEST OF GUNS N' ROSES
00695183 ....$22.95

HARD ROCK SOLOS
00695591 ....$19.95

JIMI HENDRIX
00696560 ....$24.95

HOT COUNTRY GUITAR
00695580 ....$19.95

BEST OF JAZZ GUITAR
00695586 ....$24.95

ERIC JOHNSON
00699317 ....$22.95

ROBERT JOHNSON
00695264 ....$22.95

THE ESSENTIAL ALBERT KING
00695713 ....$22.95

B.B. KING – THE DEFINITIVE COLLECTION
00695635 ....$22.95

THE KINKS
00695553 ....$22.95

BEST OF KISS
00699413 ....$22.95

MARK KNOPFLER
00695178 ....$22.95

BEST OF YNGWIE MALMSTEEN
00695669 ....$22.95

BEST OF PAT MARTINO
00695632 ....$22.95

MEGADETH
00695041 ....$22.95

WES MONTGOMERY
00695387 ....$22.95

BEST OF NIRVANA
00695483 ....$24.95

THE OFFSPRING
00695852 ....$24.95

VERY BEST OF OZZY OSBOURNE
00695431 ....$22.95

BEST OF JOE PASS
00695730 ....$22.95

PINK FLOYD – EARLY CLASSICS
00695566 ....$22.95

THE POLICE
00695724 ....$22.95

THE GUITARS OF ELVIS
00696507 ....$22.95

BEST OF QUEEN
00695097 ....$22.95

BEST OF RAGE AGAINST THE MACHINE
00695480 ....$22.95

RED HOT CHILI PEPPERS
00695173 ....$22.95

RED HOT CHILI PEPPERS – GREATEST HITS
00695828 ....$24.95

BEST OF DJANGO REINHARDT
00695660 ....$22.95

BEST OF ROCK 'N' ROLL GUITAR
00695559 ....$19.95

BEST OF ROCKABILLY GUITAR
00695785 ....$19.95

THE ROLLING STONES
00695079 ....$22.95

BEST OF JOE SATRIANI
00695216 ....$22.95

BEST OF SILVERCHAIR
00695488 ....$22.95

BEST OF SOUTHERN ROCK
00695560 ....$19.95

ROD STEWART
00695663 ....$22.95

BEST OF SYSTEM OF A DOWN
00695788 ....$22.95

STEVE VAI
00673247 ....$22.95

STEVE VAI – ALIEN LOVE SECRETS: THE NAKED VAMPS
00695223 ....$22.95

STEVE VAI – FIRE GARDEN: THE NAKED VAMPS
00695166 ....$22.95

STEVE VAI – THE ULTRA ZONE: NAKED VAMPS
00695684 ....$22.95

STEVIE RAY VAUGHAN
00699316 ....$24.95

THE GUITAR STYLE OF STEVIE RAY VAUGHAN
00695155 ....$24.95

BEST OF THE VENTURES
00695772 ....$19.95

THE WHO
00695561 ....$22.95

BEST OF ZZ TOP
00695738 ....$22.95

Complete descriptions and songlists online!

FOR MORE INFORMATION, SEE YOUR LOCAL MUSIC DEALER, OR WRITE TO:

HAL•LEONARD® CORPORATION
7777 W. BLUEMOUND RD. P.O. BOX 13819 MILWAUKEE, WI 53213

www.halleonard.com

Prices, contents and availability subject to change without notice.